Celebrate
the Legend

25 Years of Milwaukee Irish Fest
1981-2005

by Martin Hintz

Celebrate the Legend

25 Years of Milwaukee Irish Fest
1981-2005

Written by Martin Hintz
Designed by Designsmith
Published by Milwaukee Irish Fest
Milwaukee, Wisconsin 2006

Celebrate the Legend

25 Years of Milwaukee Irish Fest

1981-2005

Hintz, Martin
    Celebrate the Legend: 25 Years of Milwaukee Irish Fest, 1981-2005
    ISBN 0-9774818-0-8 paperback
    ISBN 0-9774818-1-6 hardcover

2005 Milwaukee Irish Fest Board of Directors

(l-r) 1st row: Donna Brady, Jane Anderson, Barb Tyler, Gail Fitzpatrick, Ed Ward, Bob Mikush
2nd row: Kathy Rave, Pat Russell. Colleen Kennedy, Lori Dahm
3rd row: Kevin Kendellen, Bernie McCartan, Maricolette Walsh
4th row: Tom Tiernan, Tadgh McInerny, Joe King, John Killoren, Mike Dahm
missing: Tom O'Connell

Thanks for the Memories

A history of this depth, **Celebrate the Legend**: 25 Years of Milwaukee Irish Fest, 1981-2005 could not have been accomplished without the team effort that has characterized Milwaukee Irish Fest for the past quarter of a century. The author, as well as the Irish Fest board and officers, subsequently thanks all those who dipped deep into their memory banks and reflected on how the festival has affected them and their families. Dozens of individuals waxed eloquent, contributed laughs and shared their experiences. With apologies, there were numerous fantastic stories that did not make it into this book...the only reason being the demands of space.

Special thanks is extended to the numerous photographers whose works contributed to cataloging the history of the world's largest Irish cultural event. It takes a keen eye, patience, a knowledge of the grounds and technical skill to record the hectic ebb and flow of a busy festival weekend. Among the many photographers whose work has been archived by Irish Fest, photographs for **Celebrate the Legend** include those taken by John Alley, Paul Henning, Dick Beauchamp, Barb Tyler, Mary Ann Mikush, Jane Gleeson, Mark Goff, John Nienhuis, John Walrath, Dave Denemark and Ed Ward. Other photos for this book were gleaned from the archives of The Irish American Post and the author's collection. Appreciation is also extended to readers Nick Michalski and Kathy Quirk.

For all the thousands of our Irish Fest friends -- some sung in these pages and many more unsung but still lovingly appreciated -- this book is yours.

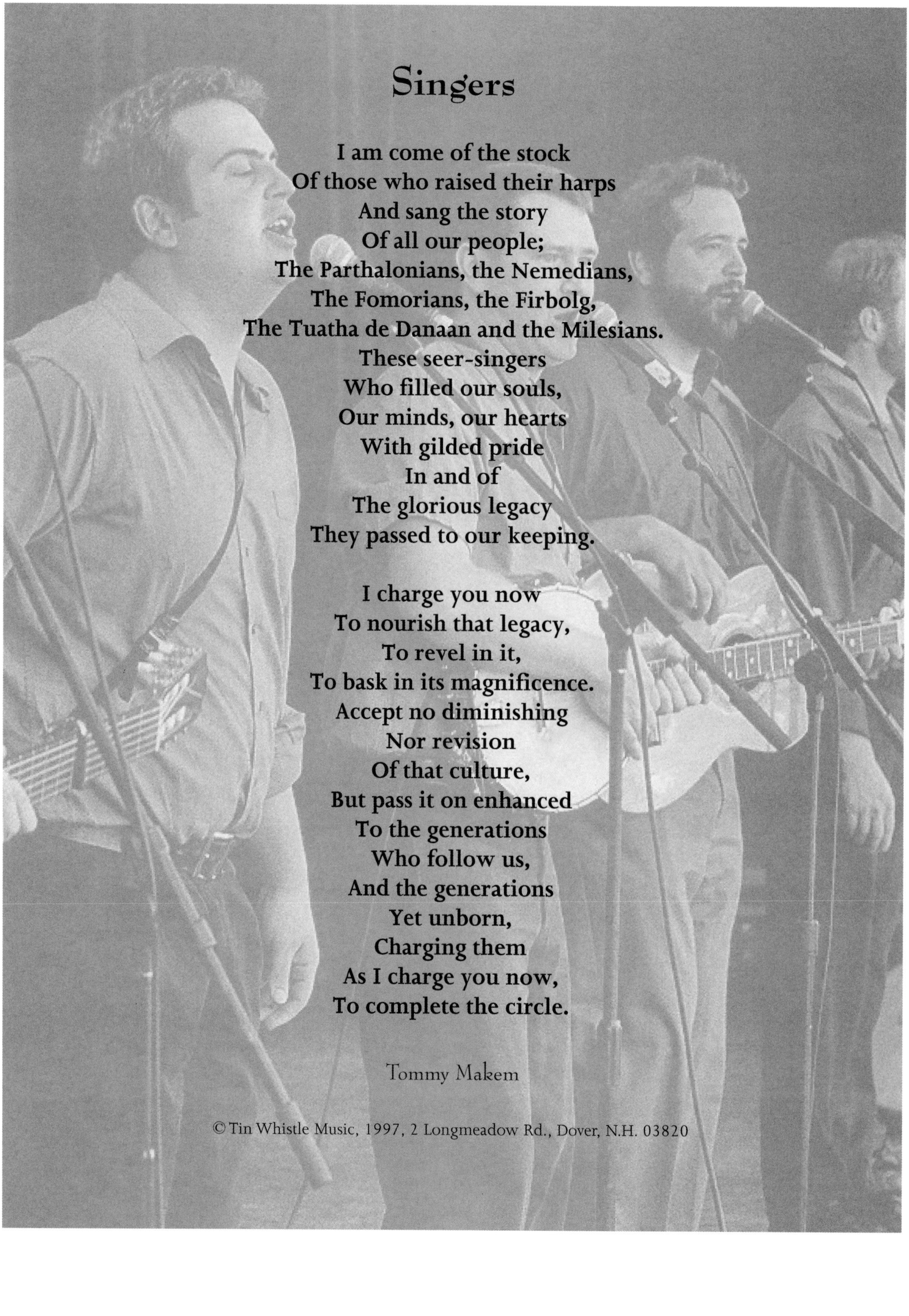

Singers

I am come of the stock
Of those who raised their harps
And sang the story
Of all our people;
The Parthalonians, the Nemedians,
The Fomorians, the Firbolg,
The Tuatha de Danaan and the Milesians.
These seer-singers
Who filled our souls,
Our minds, our hearts
With gilded pride
In and of
The glorious legacy
They passed to our keeping.

I charge you now
To nourish that legacy,
To revel in it,
To bask in its magnificence.
Accept no diminishing
Nor revision
Of that culture,
But pass it on enhanced
To the generations
Who follow us,
And the generations
Yet unborn,
Charging them
As I charge you now,
To complete the circle.

Tommy Makem

Table of Contents

Chapter 1

John Maher fiddled a tune for a very pleased Mayor Henry W. Maier during a proclamation signing at City Hall on July 27, 1981

Ode to the Old

The History of Irish Fest
1981-2005

Ode to the Old

For a quarter of a century, the best thing about summer -- in the eyes of the Celtic world -- has been Milwaukee Irish Fest. Not only is the event the *Máthair* of Irish Festivals, but it's the *Athair*, as well...the mom and pop of Irish-ness in North America.

Under the direction of Ed Ward, a local attorney and founding member of the Irish folk group Blarney, months of planning went into the first festival which kicked off in 1981. But the seeds of the festival were formed earlier, as early as 1975 when Blarney was born at Marquette University under the musical aegis of Ward and Bernie McCartan. The pair put an ad in the Shamrock Club *Emerald Reflections* newsletter that year and recruited friends John Maher and John Testin to round out the original Blarney contingent. Maher left about a year later to play with other bands.

The city's Irish music scene was expanding in those halcyon days. Feiseanna (which morphed into Gael Wind), consisted of Jeff Keeling, Martin Dowling, Dennis Abere, Pat Williams, Dan Hosmanek and John Maher. A contingent of Irish dancers also contributed their talents to Milwaukee's Irish world. Two of the major venues for traditional tunesmithing and the folk scene were Derry Hegarty's Irish pub on the far West Side and Kit and Josie Nash's Irish Castle. The latter had just opened on the South Side and quickly provided a loyal audience whenever Blarney played there. Nash's also became the site for many Irish Fest meetings over the years. According to

some wags looking back to those Goode Olde Days, Irish Fest was actually formulated to provide another steady gig for Blarney to play each August.

In 1977, Ed Ward became president of the Milwaukee chapter of the Shamrock Club of Wisconsin, with McCartan as sergeant-at-arms and Maher as treasurer. At the same time, Ward was also a volunteer office worker on the Summerfest grounds, under the direction of then-director Rod Lanser and operations manager Kris Martinsek.

Festa Italiana -- the first of Milwaukee's many ethnic festivals eventually held at the lakefront Summerfest grounds -- was launched with great fanfare in 1978. Ward and many others in the Irish community volunteered to help their Italian friends in various capacities at Festa and were able to gain insight on the internal operations of a festival. On a steamy Festa Saturday night in July, 1980, based on what he had observed over the years, Ward told a group of pals that the Irish also needed a festival of their own. He returned home that evening to excitedly tell his roommate, John Shiely, "We're going to start an Irish Fest."

To Ward's knowledge, he had never said or discussed this idea with anyone before then. "Nor did I know of anyone else who was thinking about doing something like this," Ward recalled. "The significance of that day, however, was that I had convinced myself that we could do it. And I also realized that

Ed Ward (L) shook hands with Summerfest director Rod Lanser during a lakefront contract signing ceremony on April 25, 1981.
Among the wellwishers in the background was an applauding Lorraine Murphy

In July, 1981, Mayor Henry W. Maier presents a congratulatory proclamation to Irish Fest officials Bernie McCartan, Legal Counsel, Mary Cannon, Assistant Festival Director, and Ed Ward, Festival Director

Irish Consul Conor Barrington speaks at the festival's opening ceremony on August 21, 1981. Seated behind him are Summerfest director **Rod Lanser** and Milwaukee County Executive **William F. O'Donnell**

Irish dancers were part of the opening day program for the initial Milwaukee Irish Fest

First Blarney album cover

The original Blarney in the Goode Olde Days, (l-r) John Maher, Bernie McCartan, Ed Ward and John Testin

once we started it, the risk of a failure would fall squarely on my shoulders," he said.

Ward, aided by McCartan, then began chatting up locals who had the moxie to pull off something of this dimension. Among them were Bill Drew, head of the Milwaukee Department of City Development. A former alderman and Common Council president, Drew was a "behind-the-scenes, go-to guy," in Ward's estimation. Drew's secretary, Mary Jane Champagne, also provided a great deal of assistance. Then there was Milwaukee County Executive William F. O'Donnell who had "tremendous Irish pride and intense loyalty" to his heritage and community, according to Ward. City Treasurer Jim McCann was another valuable backer.

Corporate headhunter Patrick Joseph (P.J.) Murphy was drawn in for his intimate knowledge of the business community. Miller Brewing Company executive Jerry McCloskey also climbed aboard. Lawyer-accountant Jerry Hegarty of Wolfe & Co. and Dan Steininger, president of Catholic Knights Insurance Society, were initially consulted on an Irish Fest budget. Steininger was also grandson of Milwaukee's longtime Irish Socialist mayor Dan Hoan (1916-1940), a canny politician as well as community advocate.

To help review the budget, Ward called for a breakfast meeting that late summer at the Milwaukee Athletic Club. Attending were Ed Ward, Hegarty, McCloskey and Steininger. There was clearly some skepticism at this meeting but the group agreed to proceed. McCloskey was an enthusiastic supporter from the start. Hegarty ended up doing the festival's books *pro bono* for many of those early years and Steininger has supported the festival every year through a donation by Catholic Knights and the Hoan Foundation.

The Gaelic ball really began rolling then. On September 24, 1980, Ward and McCartan went to the Shamrock Club. They informed the group that a separate corporation was being established so that the club had no legal liability if the effort failed. The club was asked for $200, more as a pledge for moral support than anything else. The Irish Fest contingent obviously wanted the only local Irish organization to be somehow involved. The Shamrock Club also subsequently guaranteed payment of the raffle prizes, as well as the costs related to admission ticket and poster printing. This amounted to a guaranty of more than $14,000. This much-appreciated guaranty was significant given the club's finances. These generous gifts of

History

10

money and club support were enhanced by the many Shamrock Club members who also volunteered their time and involved their families and friends in the Festival.

Ward and McCartan then met with the Summerfest staff to see what needed to be done in contracting with the lakefront show grounds. More brainstorming sessions quickly followed. An October 16 meeting with Bill Drew at the Harp pub along the Milwaukee River involved intense discussion about acquiring community and civic support.

The first full-fledged meeting for planning Irish Fest took place on November 25 at Margaret Hegarty's Mr. Guinness pub in West Allis. The hard work and long hours in the talk-filled back rooms here and at the city's other Irish pubs and homes of organizers would soon be paying off.

In addition, as all this was taking place, Blarney was cutting its first album, *Blarney*, at Milwaukee's Solar Recording Studios. Along with group regulars McCartan, Testin and Ward, Kevin Stapleton, Blarney's new bass guitarist, had joined when John Maher left the band.

It was originally thought that there might be a collaboration between the Gorey Arts Festival in Co. Wexford and Irish Fest. According to newspaper reports of the day, Paul Funge, artistic director of the Irish event, and Ward hoped to share artists who could perform at both shows. However, shortly after discussions started in 1980, Funge was transferred to another job and the idea died.

Ward met with the popular Irish Rovers the day following the group's concert at the Pabst Theatre on January 16, 1981, and told them about the festival. The event organizers had virtually no money at the time but had asked local bar owners Derry Hegarty and Danny O'Donoghue each for $1,000. The two were quick to help. The seed money was earmarked to cover a down payment on the Irish Rovers if they could perform at the first Irish Fest. The band was interested but later its agent called to say the Rovers were not available due to scheduling conflicts.

But no one was dissuaded from continuing the planning, even with this setback. From there, a tour of the Italian Community Center fueled discussions of the ins-and-outs of festival organization. Summerfest's Martinsek attended a board meeting on March 12 to go over the grounds contract. The festival checking account held $1,919. Martinsek said she looked forward to such Irish Fest get-togethers, most of which were held at Nash's pub. A lot of work would be accomplished, she indicated, and headway made toward a contract and plans for the first event. After the muscle work, the meetings always ended with music and often singing and dancing. Kit Nash even tried to teach her some Gaelic although, to this day, Martinsek admits that she is still not certain what she was saying. "We all figured you guys were at the beginning of a great run. There were so many talented people on the organizing group for Irish Fest, as well as a palpable enthusiasm for all things Irish that was contagious," she added.

There was always time for fun. A kick-off party was held February 21 at the Italian Community Center with performances by Blarney, Foggy Dew and Feiseanna. That event was followed by another musical blast February 27 at the spacious Grant Boulevard home of Sandy and Marty Hintz. Blarney

Derry Hegarty

Archbishop Rembert Weakland celebrated the first festival's Liturgy for Peace and Justice. Helping bring the gifts to the Pabst Stage was Milwaukee County Executive William F. O'Donnell

Helen and Danny O'Donoghue

A jovial Paddy McFest debuts at the 1982 festival

Milwaukee Irish Fest

May 21, 1981

By the Members of the Common Council, File Number 81-223. Resolution congratulating Irish Festivals, Inc., for its successful efforts in organizing the first Irish Fest in the City of Milwaukee.

Whereas, Irish Festivals, Inc. has worked diligently for months with the Shamrock Club of Wisconsin, the Neville-Dunn American Legion Post and the Irish Musicians of Milwaukee, among others, to organize the first Irish Fest in the City of Milwaukee; and

Whereas, Irish Fest provides wholesome entertainment at affordable prices, and offers an endless variety of activities that are entertaining and informative, such as workshops on traditional Irish instruments, songs and dances; and

Whereas, The Festival spotlights the City's sizable and active Irish community, and draws deserving attention to the outstanding contributions of Irish and Irish Americans to the City, country and culture; and

Whereas, Proceeds from the Festival will go toward establishing an Irish Community Center, and toward financing worthwhile activities that will benefit the Irish community and the entire City; now, therefore, be it

Resolved, That the Common Council of the City of Milwaukee herewith congratulates the ambitious and enthusiastic organizers of Irish Fest for the successful culmination of their efforts in three days of family entertainment on August 21, 22 and 23, 1981; and, be it

Further Resolved, That the Members of this Honorable Body extend their heartfelt wishes for many future Irish Fests, which act as a unique showcase for the City and its civic-minded Irish citizens; and, be it

Further Resolved, That this Resolution be spread upon the permanent Record of this Council, and that a suitably engrossed copy be presented to Irish Festivals, Inc. Adopted under Suspension of the Rules.

played at the latter, just before their new album debuted at a Shamrock Club meeting on March 5.

Intense board meetings that spring solidified use of the Shamrock Club raffle license and a public relations contract was signed with Sandy Hintz's Hintz Literary Services (eventually Hintz & Company). It was also arranged for the Neville-Dunn American Legion Post to take over the transportation sector under the direction of Chet Radtke and Tim Casey. John Maher took over as chairman of the budget committee, a poster contest was approved and prizes of gold coins for the fest's giveaway were okayed after the idea of awarding a flock of sheep and bags of potatoes was rejected in one hilarious think tank session.

The drive for volunteers -- at first led by Lorraine Murphy, Mary Otto, Jane Anderson and Jackie Kane, and later aided by sisters Barbara and Maureen Tyler -- drew in almost every Mc, Mac and O' in a four-county area and beyond. Mover-and-shaker Bill Drew took over the handling of business tickets, Jan Pergoli became food coordinator, Kathy Ferrell was named parade director, Dan McCarthy took the Red Cross duties, Jack Ward agreed to handle grounds maintenance.

Jerry McCloskey was elected treasurer. His kitchen table was to become legendary, overflowing as it was with bills, receipts, ledger paper and adding machine slips, much to the distress of his wife, Polly. Tom Cannon was to manage the cultural area. Dan Steininger sent in $250 from the Hoan Foundation to help jumpstart the coffers. Key was Mary Cannon, who was appointed assistant festival director with the responsibility of supervising all areas where revenue was generated.

A crowd of happy Irish Festians and friends attended a contract signing on the Summerfest grounds at 10 a.m., April 25. The sunshine and cloudless skies, despite the cool lakefront air, seemed the harbinger of good things to come. Fiddle music and much applause startled the resident gulls, as handshakes between Ed Ward and Summerfest director Rod Lanser confirmed the penned signatures. The first community-wide promotion was held May 30, a ceili outside the Milwaukee County Stadium. Blarney, of course, performed, along with Foggy Dew and others. The event earned $1,088 and drew in 35 new volunteers.

The organizers also applied for a $7,500 grant from the National Endowment of the Arts (NEA) Folk Arts program to host Mick Moloney's musical group, the Green Fields of America. Mary Cannon wrote the grant, which was supported by numerous local political and civic leaders. In July, the city's Department of City Development, headed by Bill Drew, agreed to sponsor the grant.

On July 27, a festival contingent presented a poster to then-Milwaukee Mayor Henry W. Maier, who signed a proclamation on behalf of the organization. More meetings followed, the adrenaline rush was rising as I-Day, Irish Fest Day, approached. On the week preceding the opening, the grounds were readied, tents put up and plenty of beer unloaded. The fest's first budget was pegged at $236,000.

Then it was here, August 21. The morning's promotional kickoff was a waiter's race outside the downtown Hyatt Hotel, hosted by Mr. Basketball,

Tracy Wayson and John Gleeson
shared a light moment with Kit and
Josie Nash

A Hundred Thousand
Welcomes to IRISH FEST '81
A summertime celebration of
the fun and excitement of
Ireland on Milwaukee's lakefront
August 21-22-23.

Derek Bell

Marquette University coaching personality Al McGuire. The adrenaline rush
was palpable by the time the gates swung open. The ensuing weekend was
alive with music, fun and even a bit of frantic scurrying as last-minute
challenges were resolved. The entire event was a sea of green under bright
summer skies. High-fives, cheers and hugs concluded the festival at midnight
that final Sunday. Golf carts packed with exhausted, but ecstatic, workers
careened around the grounds. No collisions were reported.

The finance committee presented its final report on November 11. According
to its figures, the festival was $40,000 over budget but total expenses were
$290,423, with a profit of $4,439.11. There was $12,000 in cash on hand
and $20,000 in tangible assets. Figures were fuzzy on attendance, however,
because a more accountable Summerfest turnstile gate system would not be
installed until three years later. Originally, it was estimated that 102,000
people attended, a subjective number. That initial figure was duly reported in
Billboard magazine, the show business Bible. But the number was revised to
70,000 people in the November 11 report, with an estimated 60,000 said to
be paying guests. Eventually, after auditing, it was determined that about
40,000 people actually attended the first festival.

Dennis Day

These figures notwithstanding, the board -- during its December 15 meeting
-- agreed to proceed with a festival the following year. And the Green Machine
moved ahead. Milwaukee Irish Fest has subsequently rollicked and rolled
along to its subsequent 5-, 10-, 15- and 20-year anniversaries, finally
reaching the grand 25-year mark in 2005.

The journey was not always easy. The hurdle presented by a financially
troubled second year was overcome by tight budget controls. By 1983, the
festival was on its way to being well-grounded, with $315,000 earmarked for
operations. Even with occasional rains -- such as the Great Flood Year of 1987
and more bad weather in 1997 -- careful management ensured the event's
ongoing success.

McCloskey's biggest challenge as treasurer was to bring to the board sound
recommendations to help the fest succeed financially. He really pushed for a
strict save-for-a-rainy-day policy. Several of the financial types referred to this
as "The McCloskey Doctrine."

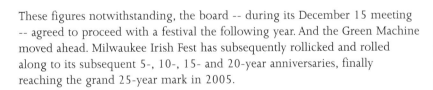

Outgoing festival treasurer Jerry McCloskey
"passes the buck" to incoming money-man
Tom Barrett in 1987

Over all this time, the festival garnered world-wide attention for the extent of its cultural and musical programming. Reviewers called the event "The Gentle Festival," "The Family Festival," "the Mother of All Irish Festivals" and the "Super Bowl of Irish Music."

A succession of committed and concerned Irish and friends of the Irish have guided the festival's operations on the board and as officers and coordinators. Thousands of seasoned and new volunteers from all walks of life have continued to pump excitement into each year's event.

The festival draws guests from around the United States and numerous foreign countries. Consistently, between 45 to 48 percent of the festival's guests are from outside Wisconsin. Irish Fest has the highest percentage of guests from outside the Milwaukee metropolitan area of any of the festivals, including Summerfest. In 1982, Irish Fest initiated summer lodging packages and worked with area hotels and the Wisconsin Innkeepers Association to develop cost-effective, financially attractive packages. In addition, the festival actively promotes itself with group tour operators and motorcoach lines around the country. The festival is a member of the Greater Milwaukee Convention and Visitors Bureau and the International Festivals Association.

Why do the visitors come? The answer is obvious. The world's top Celtic performers have entertained at Irish Fest. Many have returned several times. Included in the lineup over the years have been such stars as Tommy Makem and Liam Clancy, the Chieftains, Paddy Reilly, Carmel Quinn, John Gary, Dennis Day, the Tannahill Weavers, Schooner Fare, Stockton's Wing, Cherish the Ladies, the Wolfetones, Green Fields of America, De Danann, Frank Patterson, Danu, Afro Celt Sound System, La Bottine Souriante, Mick Moloney, Mike Cross, Battlefield Band, Touchstone, Dublin City Ramblers, Clancy Brothers, Barleycorn, Altan, Arcady, Patrick Street, Seven Nations, Natalie McMaster, Solas, Eileen Ivers Band, Gaelic Storm, Liz Carroll and hundreds of others.

There were many more in the traditional vein. Among these have been Terry (Cuz) Teahan, Bridget Fitzgerald, Gearóid Ó hAllmhuráin, Kevin Henry and Colm O'Donnell. Numerous regional and local groups also perform. A number received their first national exposure at the festival.

Among the other noteworthy performances have been those of seanachie Batt Burns, a noted Co. Kerry storyteller, and those of the Belfast Harp Orchestra. In 1992, US Steel helped underwrite "The Great American Hootenanny" in which Tom Paxton, the Limeliters and Schooner Fare performed.

In subsequent years, the Hootenanny featured the Kingston Trio, the Brothers

A die-hard fan watches the Scots-Irish Sing-off during the great flood of 1987

Four and Glenn Yarbrough. In 1996, the festival hosted the United States debut of *Island Wedding*, a concert suite by Irish composer Charlie Lennon. The Omagh Youth Choir first appeared in 2001.

Culture also plays an important role in making Irish Fest what it is. The Guinness Brewery Museum, the National Gallery of Ireland, the National Museum of Ireland, Tourism Ireland and Shannon Development Corporation have been among the many groups and organizations from Ireland assisting with exhibits.

The festival has worked with the numerous corporations, arts organizations and museum facilities on both sides of the Atlantic, including the Foynes Flying Boat Museum and Galway Crystal. Over the years, dozens of artists as impressive as Fionntain Gogarty, Rosemary McCarron, Una McDonagh and the Women's Inter-Island Network have also presented their art works. Irish stagecraft has found a receptive home at the festival, leading to the

formation of the Irish Fest Theatre by John Gleeson. The theater later spun off as a local repertory company under the umbrella of Milwaukee Irish Arts. Productions from noted Irish playwrights and those by homegrown talent are regularly performed at the festival by troupes from around the United States, Canada and Ireland. Sports such as rugby, hurling, currach racing and Gaelic football add another aspect of fun. The sports are presented under the umbrella name of the Finn MacCool Games in honor of the legendary Irish warrior-athlete. In 1987, an internationally sanctioned tug-of-war competition was added to the athletic lineup. Tugs were later named after the original organizer, Bob Sullivan, who was killed in an auto accident. From 1981 through 1988, a major dart tournament also drew competitors from more than 10 states.

From its inception, Milwaukee Irish Fest emphasized family fun. A large Children's Area includes an art contest, mini-golf on a map of Ireland, "pot of

Tommy Makem and Liam Clancy

The Druids: Jeff Grygny & Bob Zimmerman

Jack Early acted as a character from Jonathan Swift's *Gulliver's Travels* in a 1990 festival promotion on Milwaukee's lakefront

gold" games, storytellers, wandering jugglers and magicians. Red hair and freckle contests, a baking competition, the Potato Olympics, poetry writing and Irish trivia contests have continued in this spirit of frivolity.

Daily parades add another element to the weekend's schedule. In 1987, the festival's own McNamara's Band debuted. And annually, a clan reunion honors one or another of the Irish family groups. *Ceili* and step dancing demonstrations and lessons are integral to each year's program, as well. Then there are dog shows which feature most of the nine native breeds of Ireland, plus bagpiping, strolling musicians and poets.

Also around the early 1980s, County Executive O'Donnell rescheduled his annual fireworks and stroll over the Daniel Hoan Memorial Bridge to coincide with the new Irish Fest. The four-mile-long structure, named after former Mayor Hoan, spans the Milwaukee River near the harbor. O'Donnell's Bridge Walk was to become a popular addition to the festival for several years, especially since the county executive, the festival's rotund mascot Paddy McFest and Irish musicians greeted trekkers with pieces of cake at the halfway point.

Former Irish Fest presidents: (l-r) Jane Walrath, Barb Tyler, Ann Comer, Jane Anderson, Tom Barrett (former treasurer) and Colleen Kennedy

The Sunday Liturgy for Peace is another major element of Irish Fest. Cardinal Cahal Daly, Primate of Ireland, Archbishop Timothy Dolan and many other noted clergymen have been principal celebrants of the Mass over the years. Non-perishable food items collected at the Masses have been donated to area food banks. That project is co-sponsored by the St. Vincent de Paul Society, the Interfaith Conference of Greater Milwaukee and the Hunger Task Force. Irish Fest was one of the first organizations in Milwaukee to launch such a program to aid the needy. More than 36,000 pounds of food were collected before the liturgy in 2005. Since 1982, vendors have also donated unused food product at the end of each festival to Second Harvesters. Since then, thousands of

pounds of food have been contributed to the less fortunate. All of the other festivals now participate in this effort.

Each year, the fest reaches out beyond its own purview and donates prizes for fund-raisers; helps plan Irish-themed programs and encourages Irish cultural and entertainment venues. Through its Irish Fest Foundation, formed in 1993, the festival helps many civic, cultural and educational organizations in the United States and Ireland. Among the Irish Fest Foundation's outreach programs was sponsorship of the 1995 and 1996 Willie Clancy School of Irish Music in Co. Clare, Ireland. It also provided seed monty to start a scholarship fund to honor the late Paddy Clancy.

Groups representing persons with disabilities are encouraged to visit the festival. Every year, letters and phone calls are received from throughout the world seeking information about Irish Fest. The word about the festival gets out in many different ways, through advertising, news and feature stories in the trade and specialty press Stateside and abroad. The Irish Fest website, www.irishfest.com, receives thousands of hits each year.

Milwaukee Irish Fest has also become noted for its creativity, for projects that range from eagerly-sought-after collectible posters to "user-friendly" printed schedules. From the International Festivals Association, Irish Fest won first place in development of creative promotions for its 45-foot Gulliver character, which was the hit of the 1990 City of Festivals Parade and a real show-stopper on the fest grounds. The festival has also several first place awards for its schedule, poster production and public relations promotions.

In 1990, the Edward J. Ward Music Scholarship was established, with numerous awards being presented to young and old students of the Gaelic sound. In 1992, recognizing the festival's growth and need for a central headquarters, Irish Fest opened an office and information clearing house at Glenview and Bluemound Road. The move was necessary, recalled long-time volunteer Betty Mikush, because records were scattered all over the coordinators' homes. When approving the rental space, it was also decided to sublet the front to Tralee Imports, a gift shop run by Maureen Murphy Modlinski, her mother, Rose, and brother, Dennis.

A building crew was assembled to put up a wall, making the front space into the shop and the back end into two rooms. One room was an office, and the other, much larger area, became a room where the monthly general meetings could be held instead of homes and pubs. A small kitchen was built so beverages could be served during the meetings and committee sessions. The downstairs became the storage area.

In 1992, the fest also hired long-time fest volunteer Jane Mullaney Anderson as full-time executive director. Both

Irish Fest Center

actions were planned as part of the ongoing positive professional development of Irish Fest.

Within several years, it was obvious that the festival needed larger quarters. In 1998, Irish Fest purchased and renovated a Masonic temple in Wauwatosa. An official open house was held that December 10 to showcase the new facility. From that time, the Irish Fest Center has been a whirlwind hub of activity, with language lessons, children's programs, receptions, classes, music school and presentations. The John J. Ward, Jr., Irish Music Archives and library also makes the office site a true focal point for Irish information and activities.

Milwaukee Irish Fest remains dedicated to presenting the most exciting, fun-filled Irish cultural event of its kind anywhere. The positive response it has received over the years from government, the business sector, music lovers and families attests to its broad appeal.

The visit of Irish President Mary McAleese in 2005 became the jewel in the Irish Fest crown. Her much-heralded presence garnered increased publicity for the 25th anniversary year and established the event as the leading program of its kind in the world. A record crowd of 137,480 --11,000 more than 2004 -- attended the party.

The only such other major Irish political figure prior to McAleese's visit was parliamentarian and language scholar Douglas Hyde, who visited Milwaukee in 1906 and spoke to a capacity crowd at the Pabst Theatre. His audience included Governor Robert M. (Fighting Bob) LaFollette, Archbishop Sebastian Messmer and many city officials. Hyde's mission was to raise funds for *Conradh na Gaeilge* and was organized by City Comptroller Jeremiah Quinn. Hyde was inaugurated as the first president of Ireland in June, 1938.

"The strength and vibrancy of the Irish community here in Milwaukee and throughout the Midwest is at the heart of this successful festival," McAleese said to a throng gathered in front of the Aer Lingus stage on a bright, cheerful Irish Fest Saturday afternoon 99 years after Hyde's visit. "That Irish identity has endured over many generations as has the web of clan and family which holds us Irishmen and women together no matter how far apart in time or territory," she said to thunderous applause.

"On that far off island, almost everyone is related to someone in the United States," she continued. "Today, we thank God for the gift of being connected, of staying connected, the gift of community and of caring for one another and for the chance to cherish our shared kinship through music, dance, *craic* and camaraderie at the Milwaukee Irish Fest."

Obviously, the initial dream for Irish Fest is being realized.

Ed Ward shares a laugh with Irish President Mary McAleese

History

Chapter 2

It is always fun in the Irish Fest office. Left to right: (seated) Colleen Kennedy and Jane Anderson (standing) Mary Otto, Margaret Ward, Kate Walrath, Jane Walrath, Diana Stroud, Kathy Rave and Betty Mikush

Irish President Mary McAleese and her husband Martin meet festival coordinators

Doin' the Do

Volunteers

Doin' the Do

Volunteers

"I've said many, many times that the story of Irish Fest is a story about people. Boiled down to its basics, our success is really not attributable directly to good times, good music, good food, good weather. It is directly attributable, however, to GOOD PEOPLE -- creative, enthusiastic, reliable, honest and all in pursuit of a common goal."

Ed Ward, Get-Away Weekend, 2004

On April 21, 1981, Mary Otto bustled around the chairs and tables drawn up in the rear room of Margaret Hegarty's Mr. Guinness pub in West Allis. She busily handed out volunteer forms, seeking people to assist with the myriad of jobs needed at the first Irish Fest and encouraging coordinators to determine their help needs.

"Volunteers can be recruited through your contacts with friends, family, co-workers and social clubs," she emphasized. Otto pointed out that school and alumni associations and political and religious organizations were also fertile ground. "Call me at home," she offered. "That's where all of the volunteer information will be kept."

As the festival's first volunteer coordinator, Otto drew on her experience as a corporate manager, as well as a recruiter par excellence for a host of other volunteer causes she considered important. Otto knew how to cast the nets.

Her forms were specific. Volunteers were to fill their name, address, phone number and areas in which they were interested: tickets, sales or distribution; publicity, artwork, advertising; decorations for grounds; children's area, kids' games; exhibits, cultural and historical; general office assistance; volunteer recruitment; procurement and purchasing; beer sales; and special events, including contests and tournaments, demonstrations and shows, opening and closing ceremonies; and the all-encompassing "Other." There was also a line indicating: "I will help out in any area where you need me" and another asking, "Do you have any specific talents?"

That was where good friends stepped forward. Witness Bernice Reilly, the "Voice of Irish Fest." When the festival didn't have enough money for a separate phone line in that first year, Ed Ward's home phone was used and forwarded to Reilly who was on the job 24 hours a day, seven days a week. Even when Irish Fest finally got its own phone number, it was years before the event used a voice recorder because Reilly was always available. She loved talking with people from all over the world, any time of day. From the beginning, her enthusiasm and good cheer contributed to building the fest's image and reputation.

At a coordinators' meeting on July 7, 1981, Otto predicted that 300 volunteers would be needed to work the festival. She already had 270 confirmed. The list of subsequent volunteers rolled on and on and on over the next quarter of a century: Cannon, Kaye, McCarthy, Pergoli, Kane, Murphy, Walczyk, Cissne, Dahm, McInerney, Mikush, O'Connell, Tiernan, Walsh, Hamill, Walrath, Gleeson, Woodford, DeWeerdt,

First Food Collection, 1982

Gail Fitzpatrick and Bernie Beutner answering phones in the Fest office

Judy Schwerm & Jane Anderson with youth volunteers

Barb and Maureen Tyler and Monica Crotty

John Killoren

Killoren, King, Fisher, Larsen, Anderson, Mulvaney, Nazario, McManus, Heck, Mallon, McLaughlin and hundreds more.

By 2005, 4,000 volunteers were on the festival's database, representing 26 states. A brochure listing the various volunteer opportunities was also developed to assist in the recruiting process. Dozens of Youth Volunteers, youngsters learning the inside ropes of the festival operations, grew into their jobs and stand ready to take more responsibilities as they mature. Corporate volunteers have also been a wonderful contribution to the festival over the years.

Volunteers flocked to work at the fest through a variety of ways, as outlined in the peripatetic Otto's first memos. Some came for love of Irish music, others for poetry, theater and just plain fun. Most often it was friend-upon-friend contacts, as per Otto's long-ago recruiting suggestion. The process became a progression of who-do-you-know, followed up by "come on and help, and how about making 10 new friends." The response was amazing.

Even Otto's mother, Mary Keenan, got into the swing. She became the unofficial "weather committee" because she was constantly praying for good weather and sending donations to a convent for novenas to ensure sunshine, year after year. Her job was secured from the very beginning. When a soft drizzle started falling a few minutes after closing at midnight on the first day of the festival, everyone felt it was something more than the luck of the Irish that held the rain off until then. It must have been Mrs. Keenan's direct line upstairs.

As an example of the volunteer ripple effect, Jerry McCloskey, a Milwaukee Brewing Co. executive, met Blarney member Chuck Ward in an urban planning class at Marquette University and was told about the festival. McCloskey eagerly came on board to help with the event's initial planning, became one of the first treasurers and then a board president.

The energetic McCloskey also knew how to draw in volunteers, such as Milwaukee police detective Tom McKale, who assisted in tightening up security procedures and handling of currency. In turn, McKale helped organize the Emerald Society of Wisconsin, an organization of Irish law enforcement officers, many of whom eventually assisted in a multitude of tasks at the fest. Many became drivers, picking up performers at the airport, or helping with security and cash handling. It wasn't long before law enforcement personnel from more than ten cities and several states were also volunteering at Milwaukee Irish Fest. Most came with spouses and children, who also contributed their energies to making each festival a success.

Just as there are no geographical limits on drawing in volunteers, there is not an "Only Irish Need Apply" admonition at Irish Fest. The event draws in friends from many ethnic communities who also put in long, long hours. One of the hurling coordinators, Matt Larsen, is of Swedish-Norwegian-Russian descent, and the other coordinator, Karen Fink, is of German-Austrian heritage. Ina Strazdins Kielley, co-coordinator of the Gaeltacht Tent, was born in Latvia and her teammate in the Gaeltacht, Wendy Landvatter, is of German ancestry.

Mary Ellen (Melon) Wesley Jocham

Kathy Farrell

Sonya Cunningham

Underlying it all was the good feeling involving new friends trying to pull off a big event, not really knowing if it would be successful, agreed board member Pat Russell, a volunteer since 1981. For Attorney Russell, there was always a real sense of camaraderie with Irish Fest. Besides, he laughed, any group that would hold its board meetings at pubs had to be a fun group.

Barb Tyler was another first-year volunteer who learned about the festival at its inception and went on to become a board member and eventual festival president. Her background is similar to that of dozens of other Irish Fest folk who are skilled in management and are volunteer-attuned. When Tyler became Irish Fest president, she was the vice president of corporate services for a medium-sized healthcare company which was being sold. So she took a year off, traveled and performed volunteer work at a parish school near Harlem in New York. When that stint concluded, she returned to Milwaukee to set up her own healthcare benefit advocacy firm.

She and her sister Maureen, another long-time volunteer, could readily draw on their heritage for their interest in all things Irish. The Tylers' mother, Mollie Delaney, and her family came to the States through Ellis Island in 1907. The Delaneys had sailed to the States from Glasgow, Scotland, where the family had lived since emigrating from Ireland in 1847 during the Famine. On their dad's side, the sisters' Irish great-grandparents were Bridget and Patrick Dolan.

Barb Tyler's good friend Chuck Ward, a musician and festival entertainment coordinator, knew that she was on the liturgy committee at Wauwatosa's St. Bernard's Catholic Church. Ward recalled that Tyler played the guitar at Mass there and subsequently asked her to help.

Barb began assisting Mary Otto, a friend from work, while Maureen Tyler moved from the contests area to volunteers and became volunteer coordinator in 2001. Irish Fest started off so well because the initial group brought in relatives and friends as volunteers or festival-goers. These close-knit relationships lent themselves to great, often silly, times. For instance, the Tantum Ergo Club was formed as a very unofficial gathering of some of the volunteers, as a takeoff on the old Benediction hymn.

Cathy Crowley Ward

During the early days of the festival, recruiting and coordinating were sometimes casual affairs. The late Mike Clarke, who used to schedule beer volunteers, would sit down with Otto and the Tylers to fill in the bar slots with his buddies, using the Tylers' dining room as an assembly point.

At one of the meetings, another coordinator suggested that Irish Fest add an addition to the Tylers' home to accommodate the flood of paperwork. There were additional challenges. Occasionally, the coordinators received requests that a single male wanted to work with single females. Or that the females wanted to work with the males. After years of trial and error, volunteer placement operations gradually became much smoother. Today, many volunteers have been at

Bill Anderson and Liz Heck

Jerry Keeling

John Walrath

We couldn't do it without our many volunteers

Peggy & Dan Vircks

their same posts for years, a situation the coordinators are attempting to juggle. They are actively encouraging their helpers to try new jobs in order to spread out the talent pool and learn more about the entire operation.

From the first informal procedures around that long-ago table, the festival moved into the computer age. While Irish Fest's first software was purchased through bake sales, the event now has a sophisticated computer scheduling system designed by Bob Harrold, who also is a coordinator for the fest's Sunday Mass along with his wife, Paula.

To help pump up the adrenaline, kick-off parties were held at Hart Park Lodge in Wauwatosa. Organized by the late

Mike Clarke

John Kaye, one of Milwaukee's early Irish dance aficionados, these soirees drew together the ever-expanding festival family with lively music, *ceili* dancing, plenty of food, kids' activities and lots of talk.

And then, it was always crunch time. At the first festivals, Otto, the Tylers and their assistants held court in Meg's Palace, a commodious tent near Gate 6 where all the volunteers entered prior to their shifts. Well before each fest,

Katie Schaal

every volunteer had received parking and admittance passes and food coupons. Everyone then needed to log in at the volunteer tent and subsequently be directed where to report for duty.

Depending on the time of day when the crowds flooded the grounds, the coordinators regularly needed to quickly improvise staff requirements, directing volunteers to an area with the most urgent challenges.

In addition to the need to think quickly on their feet, volunteer coordinators are required to be resilient. One year in the early 1980s, the bagpipers' assembly area was situated adjacent to Meg's Palace. All the requisite tuning-up by the pipers provided, to say the least, invigorating background ambiance.

Marlene Wiseman

Another year, a pack of the Celtic Canines and their handlers gathered nearby, complete with barking, yapping and yowling by Irish water spaniels, wolfhounds, terriers and setters.

"But we persevered," Barb Tyler smiled, adding, however, "We still have residual effects from any sound that even sounds like a bagpipe. We joked about it a lot. That is one thing I can say about Irish Fest, we certainly laugh a lot."

Colleen Shannon & Skip Anderson

That good feeling continues to attract volunteers, according to the Tylers. "People come back because they love it. Even if they move out of state, they put down Irish Fest as their destination in August. It's a fun festival. They love being involved."

Judy Schwerm

Red Kennedy

Mary Pat Russell

John Moriarty

"Our volunteers are the greatest. We can depend on their loyalty and support every Irish Fest. Our festival would not be where it is today without their support. I have never met a finer group of people than the Irish Fest volunteers and I am proud to be associated with them," agreed Maureen Tyler. More than 130 of the volunteers celebrated their 25th volunteer anniversary in 2005.

A large number of the volunteers also turn their efforts into year-round commitments. In addition to working at the festival, they assist in many capacities at the Irish Fest Center, helping with the archives, working at the Green Tie and other fest-sponsored events and parties and generally making themselves indispensable in dozens of ways far away from the lakefront grounds.

As rewards for their hard work and service, a Volunteer of the Year is named annually. Three times, entire families

have been honored. Among them, have been the Robert and Peggy Hamill clan in 1994; the Rosemary and Dick Quinlan family in 2001; and the Ed and Mary Lou Heck contingent in 2004.

"(Receiving the award) was a great honor and came just months before both of my parents passed away. We will continue in their name and memory to volunteer as long as Irish Fest needs us," promised Kevin, a Quinlan son.

Five, 10-, 15-,20- and 25- year pins are also awarded to volunteers. In addition, the Chieftains Circle was to become one of the festival's highest awards. The "Chieftains" are individuals or organizations, typically sponsors or key vendors who were either helpful in getting the festival off the ground or who made a significant long-term contribution to Irish Fest's success.

Irish Fest realizes that in order to remain strong, it can not only depend

on old-timers to help around the grounds. To start developing a second-generation volunteer pool, volunteers as young as seven-years-old enjoy working with a parent. By the time the kids are 12, they are ready to go off on their own, but still with supervision.

For Judy Schwerm, youth volunteer coordinator, working with kids was a natural. In the 1980s, she helped launch Milwaukee Junior Showcase -- which included the O'Connell sisters, Shannon Murray, Mark Sweet, the Joan Rooney Strings, Kerry Stegeman, Leif and Sepp Backus and Kari and Steven Greenberg. Keith Moschea learned the Irish national anthem in both English and Gaelic. The Showcase regularly performed at the festival and other area events. In January of 1989, Schwerm became the executive director of Make-A-Wish Foundation of Wisconsin and organized a button-making booth at

A large number of volunteers turn their efforts into year-round commitments

Jack Ward

Jim Gillespie

Bill Hanrahan

Faith O'Connell

Volunteers

Tom and Nancy Cannon

Julie Smith and Bridget Smith Jaskulski

Irish Fest in 1990, which remains one of the group's most visible, and profitable, fundraisers.

The festival's youth volunteer efforts really began early. Parents and youngsters helped set up the grounds and with other festival activities. Over the years, many kids cut their volunteer teeth working inside the old King Juice stands dotting the grounds. Schwerm then began a formal youth volunteer program in 1990. At first, this was also a parent/child partnership and later evolved to kids doing things on their own. The project was an instant success. Among their projects was managing an orange juice stand on their own, sending their money back to the festival's on-site bank. There bank director Pat Brennan and the other cash-counters bemoaned, but still appreciated, the hard-earned, juice-sticky bills.

The festival quickly approved continuation of the formal youth program. Schwerm and her team designated Youth Volunteers of the Year, a program sponsored by One Potato Two. Shirts were distributed and recognition given to the kids via an on-stage presentation and inclusion in the daily parade. Up to 125 young people were involved on an annual basis, doing various tasks on the grounds such as delivering sodas and acting as runners.

The Youth Volunteer group, now headed by Liz Sanders, generally represents anyone from eight years of age through 18. The younger volunteers help their parents. The parents agree that this is great for bonding with children at a fun event, while also emphasizing the importance of volunteerism.

Festival directors agree that one of the key ways that Irish Fest will grow is with the Youth Leadership Program. Board member Lori Dahm works with youth volunteers between the ages of 13 and 18, who currently show leadership qualities or who want to become leaders within Irish Fest. The fest's main goal in 2004 was to start a mentor program between adult volunteers and these youth volunteers. As the young people mature within the Irish Fest community, they will be able to lead the other youngsters coming up behind them. "Thus, there will be perpetual growth and leadership to take over where we leave off. These youth are our next generation, who hopefully will take the festival into the next 25 years," asserted Dahm.

Jackie Kane

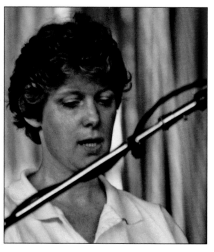
Cathy Baker Ward

Mary Shaughnessy

Kelly Brady's story is a typical tale of how young volunteers slowly assume many responsibilities as they grow within the festival structure. Brady became involved through the encouragement of his father, Mike Brady, the first beer coordinator. One of young Brady's proudest moments was in 1989 when he was named Youth Volunteer of the Year and his father was honored as Volunteer of the Year, marking the only father-son tag-team so feted by Irish Fest.

But the young man readily likes to say he became involved with Irish Fest when he was six years old in 1981, attending the very first fest. "The only thing I remember is the adults celebrating on Sunday night with lots of food and beverages. I also think there were people spraying champagne," he recalled.

Mary Cannon

When the elder Brady turned over his beer co-ordination duties to the late Mike Clarke, young Kelly helped the jovial Milwaukee barrister with the beer delivery set-up, as well as other duties throughout the fest. Brady then assisted Patty and Bruce Jensen with much the same tasks when they became beer coordinators. Later, he took over for his mom, Donna, as the recycling coordinator and then assisted with security. In 2001, he was appointed the South Hospitality coordinator.

Brady earned the nickname "Radar" from the security staff because he carried two radios when he worked for beer coordinator Mike Clarke. One device was used for Irish Fest calls and the other one for Summerfest messaging.

Keeping in the family's tradition of helping, one of Brady's favorite memories was that of his one-year-old son Jack attending his first fest in 2003. "He helped hand a soda to a volunteer. I consider this the first time he worked at Irish Fest. I believe he is one of the youngest volunteers Irish Fest has had," said the proud father.

Bruce Gondert and Tom Tiernan

To honor its thousands of volunteers from over the years, a tent was erected as the host locale for a 2005 Volunteer Clan Reunion. There, protected from the weekend's hot sun, Irish Fest alums reminisced about the "good old days," laughed about the fun they had, told silly stories, discussed departed friends and looked toward the future. A major component of the area was a photo display featuring volunteers from the past 25 years, an idea spearheaded by Cathy and Caitlin Ward. The exhibit, printed on vinyl for permanent indoor-outdoor use, was assembled by Mary Ellen (Melon) Wesley Jocham and her husband, Jay, of Hancock, Wisconsin.

Guests to the tent were welcomed by other volunteers such as Pat Carney, owner of Madison's Blarney Stone pub. Musicians such as Paddy Reilly and Tommy Makem stopped by to say hi. Visitors logged what jobs they had performed over the years, had a soft drink if they wished or simply rested their feet for a time before plunging back into the fun.

Four Eds are better than one! Ed Mullaney, Ed Mikush, Ed Ward, Ed Heck

Volunteers

25

Dale Brennan

Jan Bourke

Celtic Comments

Once the festival is over, the grounds cleared and everything packed away the Monday after the festival, the many volunteers soak their feet, perhaps take a day of vacation and then head back to their "real" jobs. But the lure of the festival remains strong and vibrant throughout year, with the clarion call echoing in everyone's head.

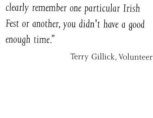

"I was under the impression that if you clearly remember one particular Irish Fest or another, you didn't have a good enough time."

Terry Gillick, Volunteer

Liz Kendellen

Cecilia Farran

Tadgh McInerney

"Everybody loves the Irish! Generally, the culture and music appeal to the Irish and non-Irish alike. We're perceived, as a 'happy-go-lucky,' friendly, warm, family-oriented and God-fearing people. In addition to having a Milwaukee-based Irish population, being located a quick ride north of Chicago doesn't hurt either. And, of course, the great organization, from those involved in running it to the hundreds of dedicated volunteers make the event a success."

Maricolette Walsh, Board Member

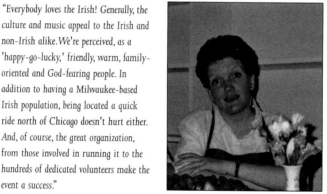

Julie Bolthuis

"Apropos of the number of Irish judges in town, I've always claimed that I run into more judges at Irish Fest than I do at the courthouse. These include Barron, Brennan, Curley, Donegan, Dugan, Doherty, Dwyer, Flanagan, Foley, McCormick, McMahon, Moroney, Noonan, Sheedy and Sullivan, to name just a few of the regulars."

Attorney Tom Cannon, Cultural Area volunteer

Veronica Ceszynski

"Milwaukee is able to host this festival because of the thousands of volunteers who give their time and also because we have a fantastic venue on the shore of our beautiful lake. The festival is extremely labor-intensive and could never survive if wages had to be paid to workers. The importance of our volunteers cannot be overestimated."

Dick Ahearn, Pre-fest Ticket Sales Coordinator

Kristina Paris

Liz Heck and Patty Jensen

"We do feel quite a sense of loss when the festival is over -- it takes a good few weeks to recover and get back to the normal everyday way of doing things. It's very sad to see good friends and amazing performers go back to Ireland, knowing that you will probably not see them again until next year."

Ina Kielley, Co-Coordinator,
Gaeltacht Tent

Bob Mikush

Joe Hughes

"Irish Fest is an excellent organization that has been successful because of a passion that its volunteers have. It is truly wonderful to watch a large group of people donate their time and efforts with heartfelt enthusiasm toward Irish Fest itself being a success as well as a successful organization. To have seen it consistently grow in size, quality and breadth of activities beyond only being a festival is evidence of such commitment from many people. That in itself is a great story."

Tom Rave, Finance Committee

Don and Carol Clark

Bill Drew

The early days were obviously much more low-key. We listened to entertainment while seated on temporary bleachers placed on the grass. My favorite story is the time we had a tornado warning and the sirens were sounding. As I tried to help people find shelter, one guest from Ireland looked at me and said, 'Does that mean we are out of beer?'"

Kathy Rave, Board Member and
Co-Coordinator (with John Moriarty) of
Travel Ireland and Irish Destinations

Pat Brennan

Pat Moschea

"Every year it is like one big reunion. I enjoy the many friendships I have made and it makes me sad that at the Scattering it soon will be ending for another year,"

Barb Tyler, Board Member

Ed Mullaney

Volunteers

27

Jerry and Sandy Bolan

Mary Lee McGinn

Lori Dahm and Dan
Banaczynski

Tom Mulvaney

Bob Harrold, Cahal Cardinal Daly, Paula Harrold

Roger and Maricolette Walsh and Tom Ament

Pat Sadowski, Jane Ward and Muriel Crowley

Sarah Dann, Colleen Kennedy and Maureeen Murphy Modlinski

Tim Benson and Vince Shiely

Mike Mitchell driving musicians

Kevin Costello and Joe King

Tanya Jones, Jamie Stroud,
Dennis Jones and Tim Stroud

Joanne & John Woodford

The Chieftain's Circle

The Chieftain's Circle is one of the festival's highest awards. The "Chieftains" are individuals or organizations, typically sponsors or key vendors who were either helpful in getting the festival off the ground or who made a significant long-term contribution to Irish Fest's success.

Chieftain's Circle 2000
Back row (left to right) Danny O'Donoghue, Derry Hegarty, Patrick J. Murphy, James McCann, William F. O'Donnell, Bill Drew, Joe Panella (Festa Italiana), Tom Ament, (front) Ed Ward, Bob Doucette, Jane Ward, Martin Hintz, Josie Nash, Cate Harris (Shamrock Club), Sandy Wright, Margaret Hegarty, Helen O'Donoghue, Dennis Boese (Miller Brewing Co.)

Volunteer of the Year Awards

Volunteer of the Year Awards are given annually to one or more hard-working helpers at Milwaukee Irish Fest, in recognition of their creativity and service in making the event such a success.

1986-1991

1986
Bernice Reilly
"The Voice of Irish Fest"

1987
Mary & Jack Early

1988
Jack Ward

1992-1997

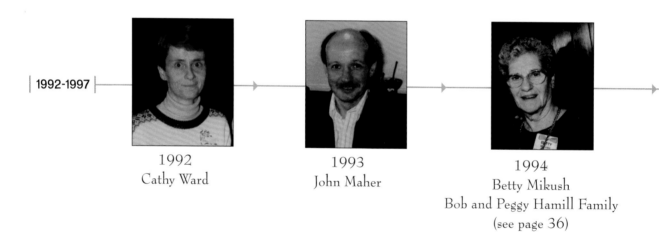

1992
Cathy Ward

1993
John Maher

1994
Betty Mikush
Bob and Peggy Hamill Family
(see page 36)

1998-2004

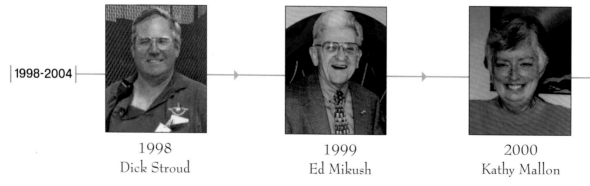

1998
Dick Stroud

1999
Ed Mikush

2000
Kathy Mallon

Volunteer of the Year Awards

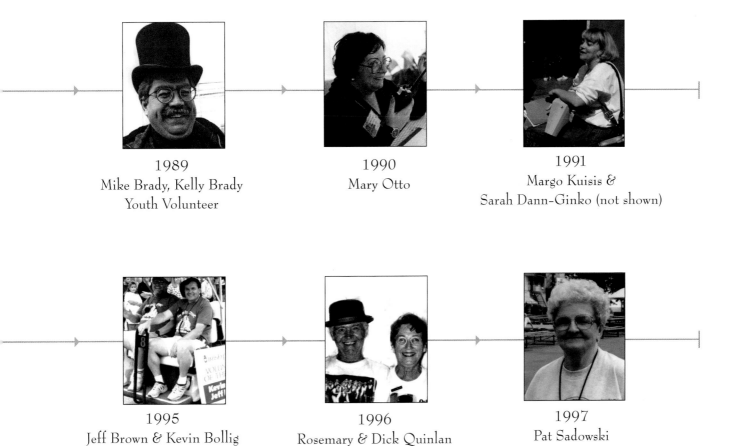

1989
Mike Brady, Kelly Brady
Youth Volunteer

1990
Mary Otto

1991
Margo Kuisis &
Sarah Dann-Ginko (not shown)

1995
Jeff Brown & Kevin Bollig

1996
Rosemary & Dick Quinlan

1997
Pat Sadowski

2001
Maureen Tyler
Rosemary & Dick
Quinlan Family
(see page 37)

2002
Jane & Bill Maher

2003
Jeanne Cissne
Ed & Mary Lou
Heck Family
(see page 36)

2004
Carol Clark

Chapter 3

Barb Tyler and Maureen Tyler

Cathy Crowley Ward, Bridget Ward, and Maureen Crowley Murphy

Makem Family Reunion
Tommy Makem and grand-
daughter Molly are flanked by
daughter Katie and sons Conor,
Shane and Rory

All in the Families

Irish Fest Clans

All in the Families

Irish Fest Clans

Open Letter to the Irish Fest Family

I have often said that I never met such a dynamic, energetic, creative bunch of people anywhere. Through your diligent efforts, we have created a unique festival unequaled anywhere in the world.

You have educated our visitors and created a thirst for more cultural and authentic knowledge. Milwaukee Irish Fest has heightened the appreciation for Irish music, drama and other arts around the world, including Ireland.

But most importantly, this huge effort has created a reliance on each other that mushroomed out into a great extended family. Throughout my involvement with Milwaukee Irish Fest, I have felt the love and support of these friendships. How lucky we are to share these bonds. We are truly blessed.

Treasure this extended family. It is a special gift and I am certain that it is unequaled anywhere.

Mary Otto, May 8, 2001
(In her last letter to her Irish Fest family before her death in 2001)

Rich, John and Tom O'Connell

The essence of Milwaukee Irish Fest, as typified by the above note, written by the always wonderfully reflective Mary Otto, the festival's first volunteer coordinator, is that of Family. With a capital "F." With her typical insight, Otto took the term "festival" and layered on philosophical, emotional and social overtones explaining what belonging to a real family entails: loving, sharing, treasuring, involving and gifting.

Beginning with the essential household unit of mom-pop-kids or whatever rainbowed domestic arrangement works, Irish Fest has taken to heart Otto's broader concept of family. Yes, as any self-respecting bard would assert, this is all VERY Celtic. The festival continues to push outward...to one of intergenerational clan, to all-encompassing tribe with births, deaths, weddings, growing up, funny stories, separations, illness, sorrow and joy. Even with occasional interpersonal bumps and grinds that occur within any such relationship, the festival has held together, has grown, has slogged through its ups and downs... and has survived.

Katie Ward Mayes, baby Aiden and Kurt Mayes

Witness the Smiths, Stephens and McLaughlins, another extended clan that figures prominently within the festival circle, with Julie Smith having been a longtime board member and an area supervisor. She and her husband, Tom, are coordinators of the drivers. Kathy McLaughlin, Julie's sister, is in charge of ticket sales and her husband, Dennis, is a driver as is Terry Stephens, Julie's brother. Julie's daughter, Bridget Jaskulski, has been Crossroads area coordinator, an area supervisor and founder of the Glencastle Irish Dancers. This bonding is obvious to discerning observers such as Éamon Ó Cuív, Ireland's minister for Community, Rural and Gaeltacht Affairs, who

Phil and Mary June Hanrahan

Families

33

The McGinnis Family was all smiles

Dozens of McCormacks gathered for their clan reunion

The Marching Mangans

has visited the festival four times. For Ó Cuív, Milwaukee remains a great place for the Irish to meet. In his mind, the closeness expressed among friends reminds him of that extended family ideal, one where everyone knows each other.

In Remembrance

When members of the tightly knit Irish Fest family go on to the Great Festival in the Heavens, everyone mourns their passing. Over the fest's 25 years, there have been many, many loyal volunteers who have earned an eternal golden pass to where the angels play Celtic harps or sing sean-nós. The festival keeps a warm place in its collective heart for all such friends as Jack Early, who managed the album booth for many years along with his family, and longtime volunteer coordinator and cultural area supervisor Mary Otto. None will ever be forgotten.

"Many thanks to Irish Fest for the tribute to Jack Early at the Gulliver site. My family and I really appreciate it. We held a family gathering there Sunday afternoon with our relatives from all over and sang his favorite songs and we all felt his smiling presence there!"

Mary Early, August 22, 2000

Dear Irish Fest Family:
I heard from family about the wonderful tribute to my mother, Mary Otto, that was in the cultural area this past weekend. Thank you. I was also directed to the website and was pleased to find posted not only the letter that she wrote to her 'Irish Fest Family' but also such wonderful tributes from Ed Ward and Brian Witt. My mother loved Irish Fest and all of those involved with it. The fest became such a huge part of her life and consequently of my life and the rest of our family.

Thank you for honoring my mother in this way. I know that she would be pleased and proud...and probably a bit embarrassed as well!

Peace!

Kathy Otto, August 21, 2001

Irish Fest Folk

There is no better way to learn what it means to be included in the Irish Fest family than to listen to some of the tales.

Tom Cannon, first Cultural Area Coordinator:
"Our three children have all worked as volunteers at Irish Fest over the years. When they were younger, we participated in and won the first two storytelling contests. We still display the trophies in our living room. My sister, Mary, has been the food coordinator since the beginning, and she served as vice president of the first Irish Fest board. My sister, Susie, comes up from Tampa every year to attend Irish Fest, as well."

Around 1990, the Cannons held a Cannon-Sweeney family reunion. "All our Sweeney cousins came out from Seattle and had an absolute blast. In addition, every year we get together with other out-of-town cousins like the Barrys, Mulroys and Newells."

Tom McKale, Security:
"One of my favorite photos is (Mike) Clarke, (Jerry) McCloskey and me posing as 'see no evil, hear no evil, do no evil.' I enjoyed family moments. The girls were along to have fun and enjoy. They did help my wife, Suzie, when she was a photographer for Paddy and Molly. My daughters, Meghan, Molly and Maureen, grew up going to Irish Fest. It was a time to clap hands and tap feet to the tunes with your cousins, friends and other relatives. Molly and her husband still attend because they live in Wauwatosa. But Meghan lives in Texas, and Maureen is now in Colorado and they aren't always able to be here."

Kathy Otto, former Volunteer:
"Mom (Mary Otto) definitely kept us busy. In the early years we did a lot of work from home such as answering the phone and taking messages, helping with mailings, sorted tickets, helped organize and store the merchandise that lived at our house for a time in the early years. On the grounds, we took tickets, worked in the volunteer tent, served soda. (Brother) Jeff usually worked at the beer tents once he was old enough, and I was forever working in the Children's Area.

"One year, I was in Irish Fest Street Theater as a leprechaun. Another year, after college, I helped on the day before the Fest, starting to monitor the gate where the merchants entered … I worked that year to help set up a display in the cultural tent, as well. Mom always kept us busy, but made it fun at the same time. We never resented the amount of time she spent working on the fest or the things she asked us to do. We loved being such a big part of it all."

Jeanne Cissne, Hospitality Coordinator:
"Daughter Becky started performing (with the Trinity Academy of Irish Dance) when she was nine-years-old. My biggest thrill here was when Trinity performed the dance drama, *Grania O'Malley*, at the festival. It had won the world championship of Irish Dance in Cork with Becky dancing the lead part. (My son) Brian, who becomes Boru for the weekend and (daughter) Rachel have usually helped with hotel stuff, like moving me in and out, and giving me an occasional break."

Mary, Kathy and Jeff Otto

Kevin, Mike and Kelly Brady

Ray Crowley, Brendan and Dennis Murphy

Ed and Mary Lou Heck Family was joined by Maureen Tyler (left) and Jeanne Cissne (center)

Bill and Jane Maher with Cathy Maher Preussler, John and Father Mike

Bob and Peggy Hamill and Clan

Becky Cissne Slaske, World Champion Irish dancer: "I was at the first day of the first hour of the festival. I had not started dancing yet so my mom would dress me in this "Irish washerwoman" outfit. Green-and-white-striped socks that went to my knees, a green dress with a white apron, and a white hat.

"When I became a teenager, my friends and I could not wait to finish with our shows so we could ride the sky-glider. We would try to pick up boys that were heading the opposite direction. We would ride for free because we would flirt with the crew that was working the ride.

"Irish Fest was three days of constant fun and entertainment. I would see people that I had not seen in a year, catch up, and say good-bye until the following year. Now I'm proud to say it is the biggest Irish festival in the world and I was a part of that for years. My mom still is. I encourage people from other cities, such as Los Angeles where I live, to visit Milwaukee the third weekend in August. They have to see Irish Fest to believe it."

Diana Stroud, Volunteer: "Irish Fest has been good for bonding our family. It is probably the one thing we all have in common, along with our Irish Fest-induced interest in Ireland and its culture and music."

Betty Mikush, Volunteer: "We (husband Ed and I) come down to the grounds on the Saturday before the festival and are there every day until the grounds are put to bed on Monday after the festival. Then it is over to the (Irish Fest) center for pizza and the gathering of very tired people for a 'job well done party.' Monday is a day of rest and with Tuesday comes the putting away of all the things that are brought from the grounds to the office, getting ready for the wrap-up. And then...another year."

Jane Walrath, former Board President: "Festival memories for the Walraths started when the kids were little, counting jujubes for the potato people, climbing on the rocks, cleaning up the grounds on the day after, dancing at the festival. Now Kate teaches Irish dance and runs all the Cashel Dennehy dance shows on the grounds. By 13, they could direct the setting up of the children's area. Mike works with Bill Anderson on grounds setup, and he and his wife volunteer throughout the year.

Even (husband) John, who used to take the festival weekend as a time to go to Elkhart Lake for races, is pretty involved. He designed and built the rainbow and new castle in the children's area, takes photos on the grounds. Our biggest problem was forgetting things at home, like dance shoes, and me staying awake on the drive home."

Veronica Ceszynski, Poster Coordinator:
"My favorite poster was the 1989 version, created by my husband Ron Ceszynski and featuring my children, who were by then dancing with the Cashel School of Irish Dance. Years later, it became Cashel Dennehy School of Irish Dance. The committee chose the poster, not knowing that it was by Ron. Because it also had the Shamrock Club Color Guard, fiddler Liz Carroll and other musicians and Paddy McFest, it really tells the story of the festival. Ron passed away in 1990. I'm so glad his artwork is part of Irish Fest.

"As the festival grew, so did my family's involvement. Daughter Jennie (now McGrath), was in the first class of beginners with Cashel Dennehy. She collected many medals during her 14 years with the school. Son John also danced for a number of years, winning awards.

"John has become a known uilleann piper and plays the bodhran and whistle. He played four times in the fleadh at Listowel, Ireland, and competed once. He

Judie and John Finnegan and Family

Dick and Rosemary Quinlan and Family

now teaches Irish music. During the 2003 festival, John was instrumental in scheduling a weekend *seisiún* for pipers which was attended by pipers from Ireland, the States and beyond."

Dennis Moroney, Volunteer:
"It is hard to believe that the years go by so fast. It seems like yesterday that (daughter) Brigid won the red hair contest at the age of two and had her picture on the bus passes the next year during Irish Fest. Now she is almost nineteen-years-old. Our youngest son, Denny, will be a freshman at Marquette High, and we have two grandkids.

"My good friend, Attorney Dan Cook, is coming back from Florida to join us at Irish Fest. He still works the festival each year even though he has retired to Florida. As you might guess, he is also a beer server."

Mike Dahm, Treasurer, Bank, Board:
"We (he and wife Lori) started dating that first full year of my involvement and she and our children have been involved ever since: 10 years for me, eight for her and her kids. We have worked together in this just as we have in the rest of our relationship, it's a great partnership. She brainstorms constantly to improve the bank operation. Our son, Dan, is now assistant coordinator of the Auxiliary Bank (the beer/wine ticket function) and loves the festival as much as we do."

Lori Dahm, Bank Volunteer, Board:
"From a purely personal standpoint, I truly treasure the friendships that my family has made with the people of Omagh, Co. Tyrone, Northern Ireland. Both of my children were previously in the Irish Fest Choir and so we had the opportunity to meet and get to know all of the members of the Omagh choir.

"To see my children on stage singing with other children who have seen such horrors -- and to have come in the name of peace -- was such a proud moment. We are still wonderful friends and have visited them in Omagh, as does my daughter now. The kids are what it's all about. They are our future. They are the future of Irish Fest."

Pat Russell, Board:
"(My wife) Mary Pat has been a coordinator of the Children's Area for many years. Our son Tim, 19, is now a stage manager for the Children's Stage and a key setup worker with Bob Hamill's crew. Jackie, 17, is a volunteer in the Children's Area and a member of the Youth Leadership Team. She is also a dancer at the festival. Patrick, 15, is also a member of the Youth Leadership Team and an all-around volunteer in many areas. Kate, 12, Mike, 11, and Sean, 6, all volunteer in the Children's Area and work with Mary Pat. We have not figured out a way to get our dog involved in volunteering yet!"

Mike Boyle, Decorations Coordinator, past Board member:
"(Daughters) Erin and Meghan know nothing else but the festival as dominant as it is in their lives every August. From their younger years, where they helped (wife) Brigid count pencils and fold T-shirts with the retail crew, or helped me, in the role of "Screw Girl" (standing at the bottom of a ladder, putting washers on drywall screws and handing them to me as I put up signs), they have grown to be invaluable members of the team.

"One of my proudest moments was the year that Erin, rather than asking what should be done, brought a couple of signs to me and asked 'I think this area is ready to go, can I put these up now?' That was met with a dumbfounded nod, and 'Yeah, sure . . .' from me. Meghan has become a de facto co-coordinator, attending meetings with me, helping

Katie, Pat, and Michael Russell

The Bill McManus Family

coordinators with their requests, and covering for me when I'm not on the grounds during setup. We were honored last year to receive an Irish Fest Volunteer Scholarship, recognizing her contribution to the festival.

"The girls grew up watching me volunteer, serving others and it naturally became part of their lives as well. They've matured into hard-working, responsible young adults, respected by the Irish Fest crew and, at times, interchangeable with me. Brian Witt has taken lately to making radio calls for 'Mike Boyle, or Mini-Me,' referring to Meghan."

Jane Anderson, Executive Director:
"Our son, Bill, is the coordinator of equipment, ordering, setup and takedown. Skip is the stage manager on the Rock Stage. Tracy helps with event planning and sponsorship. Fr. Steve doesn't have a position, but he did concelebrate the Mass with Abbott (Eugene) Hayes from his abbey in California. My brother, Ed, and my sisters, Pat and Mary, come for the festival week from Pennsylvania, Texas and Minnesota and work the festival in various roles. Ed comes early and helps Bill with setup, then drives the entertainment cart for the weekend. Pat and Mary help in retail. It's become family tradition…..a fun one at that. "They all stay at my house even if they bring extra family members. It is a very high-class bed and breakfast, minus one "B." They're very familiar with the route from the grounds to my house. They typically are my drivers to and from the grounds during the week of the fest. Believe it or not, they enjoy going on the early morning runs for media events. Also, my late husband, Andy, gave me great support. He helped with the renovation of the Irish Fest building, bartended for the general meetings and helped John Maher in the office and in various other roles during the fest. He held down the fort at home when I was gone. And most

The Anderson Family l-r, Steve, Bill, Abbott Eugene Hayes, Jane, Jerry and Tracy Anderson-Wayson (Skip Anderson, Rock Stage manager, not shown)

important, he kept me grounded!" Andy Anderson passed away just after the 2005 festival.

John Maher, On-grounds Office Manager:
"I first heard about the festival plans in the fall of 1980. Ed Ward and I lunched at First Bank and he asked me to run the bank operation for the festival. I thought it would be an interesting way to spend one weekend in August. Little did I know that it would become such a part of my life. On the issue of 'convincing' (me to volunteer), I didn't need much.

"…My parents (Bill and Jane Maher) have been active since the first festival. They sold admission tickets that year and then began managing the genealogical area. (Brother) Michael has helped in a number of ways but now he deals primarily with Mass issues. (Sister) Cathy manages the beer

Donal, Aoife, Finbar, Bobby, and Liam Clancy with friend

The Black Family: Martin, Frances, Shay, Mary and Michael Black

and wine ticket sellers and her husband, Bob Preussler, now helps in areas related to the Auxiliary Bank or cash running."

Dan DeWeerdt, Contest Coordinator, former Board Member:
"The friendships that I've established for nearly 15 years are priceless. I'm indebted to Ed Ward, Irish Fest founder, and Betty Mikush, an incredibly dedicated festival volunteer. They took me under their wings in 1991, the first year I became involved with the festival."

Kevin Quinlan, Bar Captain:
"My parents, Richard and Rosemary Quinlan, got the whole family involved back in 1984. First., we volunteered to bartend at the far north bar...My sisters and brother take care of the McSorley's Cabaret. Kathe, Maureen (who also schedules volunteers) Patti, Eileen, and John, along with their spouses and kids, continue to bartend and keep things running smoothly throughout the weekend.

"...Bartending in the old days was just a lot of fun. Being there with the family all together. Joking, singing but working hard. When they started Thursday-night activities, it was originally for volunteers. Later, they opened it to everyone. Dad and Mom volunteered us to work on volunteer night as the only bartenders. Mom made all of us shamrock vests. We'd dress in the vests, green ties and Irish Fest straw hats. Countless people asked where they could buy one of our vests. 'Sorry, only Quinlans had them.' We later had other outfits, including shamrock shorts."

Mary Lou Heck, Volunteer:
"Irish Fest for the Heck family has always been like a big family reunion. We plan the year around the dates. Jennifer now flies in from North Carolina to help manage the Tipperary Stage. It was a condition in that marriage ceremony somewhere. Timm and Liz's husband, Tom, and Erin's husband, Paul, also help on Tipperary and wherever else help is needed. It has been said (and it might be true) that they had to volunteer before they had permission to get married.

"Irish Fest is the place to see those people that you only see once a year. You see the new spouses, the new babies, the old friends. It is a lot of hugging, a lot of smiles, and a lot of memories."

Katie Ward, Retail Buyer:
"...I remember sleeping on a lawn chair in the back of the first Tipperary Tea Room run by my mom and aunts and uncles. I remember being in plays on the Children's Stage and dancing to Blarney in a snakeline through the crowds with all strangers and not being scared....How does one get so involved in the fest? Family!"

Bob and Peggy Hamill, Volunteers:
"The oldest four children began volunteering in their early teens and the youngest six have been involved as long as they can remember. Their various duties throughout the years are as follows: Pat, CDs and tape sales; Mike, bottled water coordinator; Kevin, grounds with Bob and security; Tim, grounds; Kyran, assistant in the office with John Maher; Colleen, youth volunteer assistant and Top O' the Morning Run coordinator; Sean, grounds; Brigid: grounds and signs; Bobby, mini-golf assistant, Irish Fest Youth Choir, office help and Irish Fest Youth Leadership Program; Sheila, Youth Volunteer Program, mini-golf assistant, office help and retail."

Barry Stapleton, Director, Ward Irish Music Archives:
"My brother (Kevin) played in Blarney with Ed Ward and our family was also involved in the Shamrock Club so I knew that it was something pretty big that they were undertaking. I was eighteen-years-old at the first festival and brought two of my friends down with me. We met some girls dancing in a "Conga line" which was very popular in those early years.

"Anyhow, we were drinking, dancing and carousing and ended up in a little area somewhere by where the office is now. I guess it was an area where we weren't supposed to be. Ed Ward found us and asked us what we were doing! Anyhow, he asked us to leave and escorted us to Gate 6.

"We decided to meet the girls at a local bar in Walker's Point. But unfortunately, being from Muskego and not having much experience downtown, it took us over two hours to find our car and another hour or so to find the bar, which was closed.

"So, no thanks to Ed that I could be married now with a large family! That was Irish Fest, 1981."

Cathy Baker Ward, Co-coordinator, Children's Area:
"Watching the children grow into their jobs is a marvelous gift. This is one reason that Irish Fest will continue to thrive. These young people have known each other all their lives. They will continue to carry the festival's torch into the next millennium. The fest has been too much a part of our lives to let it go. This is an extended family, you can always count on Irish Fest people."

Patrick J. Murphy,
Chieftain's Circle

Sandy Wright hugs
Pat Schmiedel

Irish Fest Friends

Patrick J. Murphy, Chieftain's Circle:
"Know that I am truly honored to be considered a part of the Irish Fest family."

Sandy Wright, Chieftain's Circle:
"Irish Fest is a special group of people. And, in our humanness, we connect, distance, take risks, goof up and celebrate the successes. The apparent success of Irish Fest is due to your experience, your dedication and -- most of all -- your humanness. So, I salute you and delight in the evolution of it all."

The Musicians

The festival has always had a focus on family groupings among the entertainers, with the musical mommas and poppas regularly performing with their children. Among the familial contingents making Irish Fest their home away from home have been the Cottars from Cape Breton, Ontario's Leahy, Chicago's Baal Tinne with Noel and Kevin Rice and Anam Ri of Milwaukee.
It has always been a multigenerational approach. The members of Cherish the Ladies were reunited in 2000 with their fathers at a special "Fathers and Daughters - Music to Cherish" performance. The dads of Liz Carroll, Joannie Madden and Mary Raftery were among those participating. In 2003 and 2004, the Barra MacNeils -- Kyle, Lucy, Sheumas and Stewart -- have played on one stage while their younger siblings, Boyd and Ryan, have played with the Celtic Rock band Slainte Mhath.

As the groups mingle at the festival to talk shop, discuss new recordings and compare songs, this process also encourages a sense of belonging to that Irish Fest extended family, albeit a musical one, as Liam Clancy pointed out. The gatherings of the Clancy family also provided some magic moments. In the late 1980s, some of the finest and most memorable song sessions at the Park East hotel were those led by Liam, Tom

and Pat Clancy in the rooftop bar. In 2000, Bobby Clancy and his daughter, Aoife, joined Liam and his son Donal and cousin Robbie O'Connell for a series of shows.

The elder Clancy, who has appeared at Irish Fest with partner Tommy Makem, as well as solo and with his famed brothers, fondly recalled standing in the back of a Cherish the Ladies concert, trying to be inconspicuous because his son, Donal, a guitarist and founding member of Danú, was on stage with the group. "Joannie (Madden) spots me and calls me up on stage. What am I going to sing?" he remembered thinking as he made his way up front. But it all worked out and the joint performance with father, son and friends brought down the house.

And as the performers meet their many Milwaukee friends year after year, that "family" aspect of the fest continues to ripple ever outward. Of course, relationships between the musicians and Milwaukeeans always make for good stories. In 1991, on their first visit to the festival, the McPeakes of Belfast -- consisting of Francie, Francis, Eugene and band member Paul Burns -- stayed with Milt Parlow, a neighbor of fest volunteers Phil and Mary June Hanrahan. Parlow was very welcoming and generous during the week and the contingent enjoyed lounging around his pool at day's end. They also loved Parlow's powder-blue 1970s Cadillac that uttered "Moooo" when the horn was beeped.

When Parlow's lawn man, Lonzo, needed a lift to the bus, Francie McPeake volunteered to take him to the stop. The gang happily piled in the Caddie with Lonzo for a little spin. A couple of hours later, Parlow called to tell the Hanrahans that the errant Belfast contingent was not home yet and he was very concerned about his car. The locals held a conference in Parlow's driveway, pondering a search party, prayers or police, when they heard "Moooo." Francie described his

Brian Grinwald, Celia Farran and Cecilia Farran

Families

Chris and Martin Dowling jam up a storm

A Sunday night *sessiun* at the Park East Hotel in 1982 included (from left) Jackie Daly of De Dannan, the Chieftains' Sean Keane and Cathleen Rice. In the rear was Noel Rice of Baal Tinne

adventure and was asked how he found his way home. In his great Belfast accent, he replied, "Oh, it was all lefts and rights." Michael Black sang and played in the Cultural Village in the 1980s. As a childhood friend of Dublin-born fest volunteer John Gleeson, Black and brothers, Shay and Martin, were in and out of Milwaukee a few times at other venues and had also stayed with the Hanrahans.

When the Black Family -- reunited with sisters Mary and Frances in 1997 -- was invited to play the festival, it was therefore not a complete shock when Michael called the Hanrahans' and said, "We are trying to choose a place where we can get together and practice for a few days before the festival, and, well, we were thinking of, um, your house, Mary June." Naturally, she responded that the visit would be wonderful.

One feature that makes the talented Leahy's Luck so unique is that its members are all related. Brothers Tom and Brian Leahy front the band with bass, guitar, and vocals. Brian's daughters Michelle, Sarah, and Caitlin play violin, tin whistle, flute, and add vocals. Tom's daughter, Maura, sings and plays accordion and keyboards, and his son Evan plays the bodhran.

For Tom Leahy, the festival has been a broadening experience for the Wisconsin-based group. "Since we are a family band starting off with children at age eleven, they have improved beyond what we could have conceived...and in unexpected ways," he pointed out. "Evan started out as the little drummer boy and turned into a bluegrass guitarist and singer. Caitlin started out with mostly a forced smile but blossomed into this woman with a gorgeous enveloping voice! Just to mention two! Brian and I, the chronological adults, have already peaked and are just trying to hang on. Not sure when we get demoted to roadies."

"I've heard many times from performers that they love playing the fest for many reasons but in large part because

they are treated so well and everything is done so professionally. The festival has certainly grown in scope and it is a business. But, it is a business run by people who do everything very well but never forget the performers or the public. It is still like family, just a much bigger one," noted Kathy Schultz, promoter for Schooner Fare and a longtime Summer School volunteer. "We have more friends among our fan base in Milwaukee than almost any other city, due to the fact that when we played the festivals, we were in town for so long (four days the first time, six days the second) so we just got to know locals much more then we usually do," said Chris Jonat of Clumsy Lovers. "Each time we come back to anywhere near Milwaukee (Madison, Racine, Chicago), we get to see people we became friends with at Milwaukee Irish Fest and it reminds us what a special place that is."

Naturally, many musical families made return visits to Milwaukee for the 25th anniversary celebration. Among them were Tommy Makem and his son, Rory, and the Black Brothers (Shay, Michael and Martin). Even Ed Ward's delightful daughter, Caitlin, a member of the Irish Fest Youth Choir, performed on stage with the festival's founder and her Uncle Chuck during Blarney's 30-year reunion show.

The Dowling clan is another active ingredient contributing to Irish Fest's success. Irish-born Joe was appointed the first treasurer of the Irish Fest board but did not serve because of a bout with heart by-pass surgery. Yet he and his wife, Betty, have volunteered every year at Irish Fest. They were primarily interested in the information booths because it gave them the opportunity to meet and greet the festival goers. Joe also was the first winner of the limerick competition.

When the Dowlings arrived in Milwaukee in 1971, they joined the Shamrock Club and it was through that association that they became involved in Irish Fest. Capitalizing on a long family lineage of champion musicians back home in Ireland, all their children have enough musical background to entertain on their own.

Son Jode performs with his wife, Kate, as The Dowlings, with Jode also a member of the Doon Ceili Band and an instructor and co-director of the Center for Irish Music at the St. Paul Conservatory of Music. He has regularly performed at Irish Fest with The Clumsy Lovers and The Minstrel Druids. But best of all, he and Kate met at the Irish Fest Summer School, where Kate had been a long-time teacher. She is director of the Center for Irish Music at the St. Paul Conservatory and has performed at Irish Fest as The Dowlings and with Baltiorum and Scoil Baal Tinne.

Both of Jode's sisters have also been active in Irish music with Theresa being an exceptional Irish dancer. Christina is a singer who also had a solo show which was a high point of her Irish Fest experience, being inspired by the great music at the festival and by meeting many great singers, especially Mairead Ni Mhaonaigh, Mary Black, Dolores Keane and Niamh Parsons. In 2005, their brother, Martin, was in the second of a two-year sabbatical from working with the Northern Ireland Arts Council, while co-ordinating a project with University College Dublin. He and his wife, Chris, continue to to be very involved in the Belfast traditional Irish music scene, augmenting many years of promoting such music in Milwaukee.

Clan Reunions

Clan reunions are another fun family component of the festival, both with "officially" designated groups and informal get-togethers. Coordinator Cate Harris has been the Irish Fest representative working with family groups to make successful reunions. She provides literature assembled by former reunions and has all the information necessary in ordering food, securing easels for displays, setting up coffee urns and arranging a myriad of other details as she walks an estimated "one thousand miles over the weekend."

Many families have been honored over the years, including the McGinnitys (1990), Keanes (1991), Hanrahans (1992), McCormicks (1993), Gallaghers (1994), Delaneys (2000) and McAteers (2001). All past volunteers were hosted at their own "clan" reunion in 2005. The families have a special area where they can gather for memories, showcase photos and brag about grandchildren. Each year, the honored clan is featured in the parades around the grounds, with many in the various contingents sporting custom-made T-shirts or hats.

"In 1994, our Gallagher relatives had a family reunion at Irish Fest in the area set aside for that activity," said Jean Bills of Celtic Women International. "About 100 of us joined in the daily parades carrying little banners (and a large one) that said "Gallagher." Our family brought two of our cousins over from Achill Island for the reunion with their relatives in the United States. It was a wonderful reunion, getting to know the relatives from Ireland. I now visit these cousins every time I go to Ireland. We are all family," she said.

The Quirks hailed from Co. Tipperary. In the 11th and 12th centuries, before the Anglo-Norman invasion, the O'Quirke family was of kingly rank, ruling over a considerable territory sometimes called Quirk's Country, explained Therese Quirk who helped on the Quirk reunion of 1997. For her, the gathering was a "wonderful once-in-a-lifetime experience," attended by about 200 persons, ranging in age from a few months to more than over ninety-years-old. Family attended from around the States and as far as England and Canada.

Obviously -- from the opening Gathering of the festival to the Scattering, the last performance where musicians gather from around the grounds for one last tune -- the Milwaukee Irish Fest family remains tightly knit.

Mike Walrath, a second generation volunteer, with nephew Aidan

Joannie Madden and her dad, Joe

43

Play It Again, Sean

Music and Dancing

Play It Again, Sean

"No matter what it is musically, you'll find it at Milwaukee Irish Fest. If that doesn't happen, you're sitting in a corner."
                                                            Bill Margeson, music journalist

The heart of Milwaukee Irish Fest is music, lots of music. And that's official. Witness the festival's original mission statement laid out in its corporate statement of 1981:

Irish Festivals, Inc., is a nonstock and not-for-profit corporation formed under Chapter 181 of the Wisconsin Statutes. The purposes of the corporation are: to plan and carry out a festival known as Irish Fest, featuring exhibitions of Irish crafts and performances of Irish music, dance and literary works, so as to increase the public's knowledge and appreciation of Irish culture and its contribution to the American way of life.

As such, the festival was at the forefront of a wave of heritage awareness explained in 1980 by sociologist and author Fr. Andrew Greeley. He made a bold prediction that there would soon be an explosion of Irish American culture. Fest founder Ed Ward agreed with Greeley in a presentation made May 7, 2003, at a "Re-imagining Ireland" conference in Charlottesville, N.C.

"That prediction (of Greeley's) turned out to be true," Ward told the assemblage of Irish and Irish diaspora leaders in the entertainment, cultural, political and business worlds.

Ward continued: "Over the next 20 years, there was a definite move toward higher levels of self-conscious Irish identification. The emergence of Irish music in the 1960s and 1970s proved that Irish bands and Irish music could be successful commercial entities. And just as Columbia and Victor record companies had recognized this in the early 1900s, the ability to sustain a market for Irish music, so too did many Irish organizations and music promoters recognize a growing interest in Celtic music and recordings. In the early 1970s and early 1980s came a new and significant development that would provide a new conduit for promotion and preservation of Irish and Irish American culture: the Irish festival."

Ed Ward, Tom Paxton and Margo Kuisis at the Great American Hootenanny

Tom Rowe, Steve Romanoff and Chuck Romanoff of Schooner Fare gather with their Trinity Dance friends in 1989

Cashel Dennehy Academy of Irish Dance, 1989

Kevin Burke and Micheal O'Domnhaill

Chuck Ward, Dennis Murphy, and Kevin Stapleton of Blarney

On stage, De Danann (l-r) Johnny (Ringo) McDonagh, Charlie Piggott, Frankie Gavin, Jackie Daly, Alec Finn, 1982

The festival often themes its years. For instance, in 2000, it was "Live the Legend," with dozens of groups such as Moving Cloud, the Irish Rovers, Great Big Sea, Lunasa, Tommy Makem and the Blarney 25th-Year Reunion. In 2002, "The Sound of Tradition" held sway, with such stalwarts as Cherish the Ladies, Paddy Reilly, Dermot Henry, Carmel Quinn and the Makem Brothers. Even the classic 1960s Highwaymen were back on the road.

In 2005, the heralded concept was called "Celebrate the Legend," with a Celtic Roots Stage marking the influence of Irish culture on popular Irish music. David Kincaid tapped his talents as a musician and Civil War historian to perform songs from that terrible conflict. The lst Brigade brass band augmented his presence, performing on antique instruments. Mick Moloney explored the backgrounds of Edward Harrigan and Tony Hart, considered the fathers of musical comedy. Grammy nominee fiddler Bruce Molsky linked Irish sounds with African and blues influence to showcase the music of Appalachia. A "George M. Cohan Revue" was written and directed by Chip Deffaa, jazz critic for the *New York Post*. A tribute to Bing Crosby by historian Bob Pasch, plus appearances by musicians Carmel Quinn, Liam Clancy, the Canadian-based Garrison Brothers and Salt Creek, a bluegrass band, rounded out the "music of the generations" presentation.

Thus, from its inception, Milwaukee Irish Fest was able to capitalize on what would be a growing number of Irish musicians eager to find outlets for their talents. As it expanded, the event would become a leader in an ever-growing festival field, the "must-be-at" occasion for the traditional, as well as folk, rock, New Age, Afro Celt and other constantly morphing forms of the burgeoning Celtic sound.

Playing at a Milwaukee Irish Fest stage became the Irish music cachet. The list of entertainers is a roster of the famous and soon-to-be, with such marvelous female stars as Mary McGonigle, Aoife Clancy, Liz Carroll, Annette Griffin, Joannie Madden, Eileen Ivers and Mary Black adding their luster to the solo magic of Paddy Reilly, Charlie Piggott and Danny Doyle. The thunder of groups echoes over 25 years: De Danann, the Tannahill Weavers, Lunasa, Danú, Gaelic Storm, Leahy, Barley Bree, Different Drums and Seven Nations.

"When the Milwaukee Irish Fest started, I don't know if the organizers realized the cultural value of the enterprise they were starting," said singer Tommy Makem. "But whether by good luck or by very enlightened thought, they struck a very deep and brilliant vein of music, poetry and dance just waiting for a catalyst to send it soaring. The Irish Fest organizers -- by their excellent taste and commitment -- have proven themselves the most outstanding catalysts in

Carmel Quinn

Natalie McMaster and Sean McGuire

Steve Twigger of Gaelic Storm

their field in the world. It can be truly said that the Milwaukee Irish Fest has often been copied but never equaled. Long may it reign," he said.

Why the success of Irish Fest? The question can easily be answered in a comment made in 1998 by entertainment coordinator Chuck Ward. Speaking with *Shepherd Express* reporter Jennifer Vercauteren, Ward felt the festival's diversity was enthralling. "All categories of Irish music will be presented here, so visitors are bound to walk away with feelings of fulfillment," he said. "From old favorites like the Irish Rovers to energetic traditional groups like Dervish to the Celtic rock sound of Brother, you'll find it."

That breadth of musical offerings became the festival's signature, its cultural plus, its calling card. Indeed, in its first 25 years, Irish Fest has led thousands of patrons on a long musical journey with many wonderful twists and turns. Looking back over generations of performances, the allure of that entertainment variety continues to draw the fans. Whether the musicians are considered major talent or up-and-comers, they all have one thing in common: Irish spirit. Regardless of where they perch on the musical wire, singing low or singing higher, Milwaukee Irish Fest has given each a voice and a presence.

"But why Milwaukee?" Shay Black of the Black Family was asked by *Milwaukee Journal Sentinel* pop music critic Dave Tianen in a 1997 story. "It's because Milwaukee is special. It's the biggest music festival on the planet. The biggest in Ireland is probably 60,000, so this is very special. I think the people in Milwaukee have a genuine interest in Irish culture and music. I don't think there's a festival in Ireland that could compare with Milwaukee."

"Most of the musicians I talk to consider Milwaukee Irish Fest one of, if not the, pre-eminent festival of its kind. Many of them consider it basically the 'Big One,'" affirmed Chris Jonat, bass player and de facto bandleader of The Clumsy Lovers. The group performed in 2002 on the Leinie's Celtic Rock Stage, and then in 2003 on the Old Style/Pabst Stage.

Flute player Joannie Madden enthused in a letter after her 1992 Irish Fest appearance with Cherish the Ladies that "everyone was their most congenial and jovial. Things ran the smoothest that I've ever seen. Our soundmen were incredible, which allowed us to play to our full potential. We play everywhere and Milwaukee is the best!"

Among Our Musicians

1981
Carmel Quinn
Irish Brigade
Green Fields of
America
De Danann
Joe Feeney
Kevin Burke &
Micheal O'Domnhaill
Noel Rice
John Gary
Red Clay Ramblers
Gilmour Brothers
Blarney
Mary Ann Miller
Irish O'Leary
Foggy Dew
Gael Wind
Fiddler's Green
Brian & Marty
Grinwald
Milwaukee Junior
Showcase
Geary Irish Dancers

1982
Tommy Makem &
Liam Clancy
Tannahill Weavers
Paddy Reilly
Baal Tinne
Lughnasa
Chieftains
Touchstone
Schooner Fare
Mary McGonigle
Old Triangle
Joe & Antoinette
McKenna
Trinity Irish Dancers

1983
Dennis Day
Boys of the Lough
James Keane & Robbie
O'Connell
Thady's Remedy
Mike Cross
Irish Tradition
Cashel Irish Dancers
Samradh

1984
Dermot O'Brien Trio
Stockton's Wing
Kinvara
Dublin City Ramblers
Clairseach
Mulligan Stew
Shuffle Creek
Dancers

Music & Dancing

Seamus Kennedy   **Hal Roach**

Donny Golden and his sister Eileen

The Tannahill Weavers tune up

"(We) have attended numerous festivals here and in Ireland and Europe, both as performers and as spectators, and nowhere have we come across one with such a combination of successful qualities as Milwaukee! Not only was the setting perfect, the planning and organization flawless, and our every need attended to, but the people that we dealt with on all levels were fantastic!" said Charlie and Ann Heymann of Clairseach.

"I can't think of a better place to be on the third weekend in August," agreed John Murphy of the Irish Rovers, citing the camaraderie with other musicians and the interest in each other's performances. "Milwaukee has always been great fun," Altan's Mairead Ni Mhaonaigh admitted. "The (Irish) Festival has always been great, too, especially in regards to meeting and playing along with other musicians. And who could forget the heat, my goodness."

Chuck Ward's first Irish Fest performance was with Foggy Dew on the old Schlitz Stage in 1981. "I was scared to death, and remember that the three of us wore matching green-striped shirts! I must say that 25 years later, I get the same rush from performing on a big stage with a big sound system. It is so different than singing in the pub and seems to better legitimize Irish music."

Maurice Lennon, one of the original members of Ennis' Stockton's Wing, heard about Irish Fest from other enthusiastic performers. When the band arrived to play in 1984, it was immediately impressed with the layout and the organization. It played again in 1985, lured not only by the fact that -- as Lennon joked -- "females found the need to throw items of clothing in our direction," but by the camaraderie with the other musicians and the interest taken in each other's shows. The festival and the after-hours jamming at the Park East Hotel meant almost all-day and all-night music. "Milwaukee is now one of the top festivals in North America, so to perform there is always important to one's career," continued Lennon, an award-winning fiddler.

"Roguery was thrilled at the opportunity to play in Milwaukee again and enthralled at the incredible hospitality shown by Irish Fest staffers. There are no words -- neither mine nor Roguery's -- to describe what your organization has accomplished and how it gets better and friendlier every year. It has taken on a life of its own, and one to be revered, at that," agreed Kevin Quinn of the Omaha-based band.

"The scene here is unbelievable," singer Luka Bloom told reporter George Houde of *The Irish American Post* in 2004. "Dancing, pipes, drums. We arrived Friday and after three days, I decided to do a chill-out show, a Celtic chill-out zone."

"It worked," wrote Houde. "Drawn by his rich voice and his wonderful guitar work, the audience followed Bloom into

Liam Clancy

Sarah Allen of Flook

Mairin Fahy of Reel Time

Patrick Ball

the zone, entranced by the Irish singer-songwriter-poet. Some may have nodded off briefly. That the moon was rising over Lake Michigan with a gentle breeze kissing the shoreline only 100 yards away made the performance even more memorable."

Musicians report back to their management with comments, such as "well-organized" and "yes, not enough good gigs as this in stature and experience with the audience," agreed agent Jim Fleming of Fleming & Associates in Ann Arbor, Michigan. His stable includes Maura O'Connell and The Clumsy Lovers.

"The audiences are amazing at Milwaukee Irish Fest. I think people come from all over the country. They've heard so much about Irish Fest that when they get there they only have one objective in mind and that is to have a great time. People usually come to all three days if they can because there is so much to see and do," pointed out Patrick Murphy, who does vocals, accordion, harmonica and spoons for Gaelic Storm.

"Irish Fest has really helped keep the music alive," asserted Liam Clancy, a regular performer since his first appearance in Milwaukee in 1982 with Tommy Makem. "The festival accommodates everything from Irish rock to *sean-nos* singing. It's all magical. I roam from tent to tent to see what others are doing," he said. "Milwaukee presents such a huge platform for music. It's also a great venue for reinventing songs. People like to hear new things."

"Milwaukee is the only crossroads of its kind, including in Ireland, where people like ourselves can all meet. It's where older, established musicians such as the Chieftains and ourselves can get together with each other and with younger performers. Now that's one of the most memorable aspects of Irish Fest," Clancy continued. "Those meetings over breakfast! Great discussions."

In addition to highlighting individual performers on stage, the festival has also ardently sponsored themed original works. These productions manifested their own individually wonderful characteristics. In 1991, Milwaukee composer Sigmund Snopek II produced a fugue based on research done by local writer/actress Margaret Rogers featuring the "Sirens" chapter in James Joyce's monumental work, *Ulysses*.

Another seminal piece was the United States debut of *Island Wedding*, a concert suite written by one of Ireland's most celebrated composers, Charlie Lennon, and presented at the fest in 1996. The suite, performed by the Concord Chamber Orchestra of Wauwatosa, blended a classical orchestra with traditional musicians. Lennon's soul-searching story told of a love that was lost and then gained off the coast of western Ireland. Concert guests included champion Irish fiddler Liz

1985
Barley Bree
Battlefield Band
Terry Sexton &
Bill Crowley
Scartaglen
Judy Pintar &
Malcolm Smith
St. Jane's Gate
"Cuz" Teahan
Jimmy Kennedy
Noel Henry's
Irish Show Band
Batt Burns
Pat's People

1986
Mary Black &
Dolores Keane
with De Danann
Clann Na Gael
Mick Moloney,
James Keane &
Robbie O'Connell
Cahal Dunne
Patrick Ball
Dave Kenney
Boxty
Jamie O'Reilly & the
Rogues
Tarbolton
The Minstrel Druids
Metamora
O'Sullivan & Leahy

1987
Annette Griffin
Parting Glass
Tim Britton
Carol Hunnert
Jerry Harrington
George Doherty
Anne Johnson
Dingle Spike
Leahy Family
Celtic Wind
Arranmore

1988
Puck Fair
Cherish the Ladies
Capercaillie
The Wolfe Tones
Barleycorn
Ossian
Patrick Street
Liam Donnelly
Kim Robertson
The Johnny Gleeson
Band
Texas Lone Star Ceili
Band
Tommy Moran
Danny Doyle
Pat Roper

Music & Dancing

Edward J. Ward
Music Scholarship Winners

1990
Maria Terres-Sandgren
1991 John Ceszynski
1992 Chris Buckley
1993 Ed Palouchek
1994 Summer Curtis
1995 Brett Lipshutz
1996 Phil Rubenzer
1997 Holly Kolanko
1998 Asher Gray
1999 Brigid O'Sullivan
2000 Devin Shepherd
2001 Aislinn Gagliardi
2002 Devin McCabe
2003 Aaron Fallon
2004 Kaitlin Hahn
2005 Pat Roe

John Maher with Maria Terres-Sandgren

John Ceszynski receives his scholarship check from Ed Ward

Eileen Ivers and John Doyle

Music & Dancing

Carroll, as well as local notables John Ceszynski, Brett Lipschutz, Dave Delgado, John Nicolson and Áine Meenhagan.

Such interlocking links with the home country contribute to the importance of Irish Fest. Appearances by major groups, while not being political per se, demonstrated concepts of peace and reconciliation that remain integral to what Irish Fest is all about. The 1992 festival hosted the Belfast Harp Orchestra, brought to Wisconsin by the Republic of Ireland and Northern Ireland. It was one of the first such joint cultural efforts sponsored by both governments. The Milwaukee appearance was the only program given by the orchestra outside Europe.

Since its beginning, one of the festival's purposes has been to ensure that young musicians have a great opportunity to mingle with the world's best professionals. One of the most popular ways to participate is through the Irish Fest Choir, launched in 1988.

According to choir co-founder Pat Moschea, who is now the coordinator and producer of the choir, young adults from more than 25 different high schools have participated in the Irish Fest Choir, including young people from Milwaukee, Oconomowoc and even Illinois. The choir members come from both public and parochial schools. The choir's first performances were on the Children's Stage and eventually moved to larger venues as its audiences grew. The choir now even has its own small band. Created to promote an interest in Irish music among young people, the Irish Fest Choir was born out of the creative ashes of Randy Swiggum's music and Kate Reilly's play *Meg's Gold*, which was performed at Irish Fest. Swiggum wrote the music and directed the play. That first undertaking suggested that more opportunities should be available to include young Irish Fest volunteers and other young people in productions involving music. Over the next couple of years, there were many kids from the North Shore area, especially Whitefish Bay High School and Homestead High School, who wanted to do something in music. So it was decided that a choir might be the best way to go.

The first seedlings of a choir were sown in Swiggum's classroom at Whitefish Bay High School. He never officially directed the choir, but his presence and creative leadership suggested that such a thing was possible and could contribute towards educating young people on the merits of Irish music and Irish song. The original director of the choir was Rebecca Winnie, who has been the Homestead High School choir director for 22 years. Pat Moschea asked Winnie to be the choir's director after *Meg's Gold*.

Following Winnie as the director of the Irish Fest Choir was Todd O'Connor, who had originally been a choir member. He sang baritone in the choir in 1988, the year of the choir's founding, when he was a senior at Whitefish Bay

Paddy Reilly

High School. Recruited by Swiggum, O'Connor went on to undergraduate study at Wheaton College Conservatory of Music in Wheaton, Ill.

During those years, he returned home to Wisconsin during the summers and accompanied the choir on piano under Winnie's direction. Following Todd O'Connor was Amanda Moschea, the daughter of choir co-founder Pat Moschea. Amanada is assisted by college pal Amy Baker.

"The most fun of Irish Fest is to see how excited the kids get before a performance and how they all feel after a great concert," said current choir coordinator Pat Moschea. Numerous young choristers have gone on to musical careers as performers, teachers and

Australia's Brother hams it up

Combined Irish Fest Choir and Omagh Youth Choir

1989
Roguery
Croabh Rua
Brendan Grace
Frank Patterson
Carlton Irish Show Band
Clancy Brothers with
Robbie O'Connell
Dooley Brothers
Armagh Rhymers

1990
Blarney-15 year Reunion
Altan
Castle Rock
Full Shilling
Listowel
McTavish
Midnight Court
The Drovers
John Dillon Band
Boxty
Sean O'Neill Duo
Ceol Cairde
Dennis Doyle
Black Velvet Band
James Kelly & Mick Black

1991
Johnny Reidy Band
Storm
Rounders
Tip Splinter
The McPeakes
Roisin White
Third Man
Murphy & Douglas
John Campbell &
Len Graham
Glenghillies

1992
Arcady
Tom Paxton
The Limeliters
John McNally
The Rankin Family
Barleycorn
Bill Young
Belfast Harp Orchestra
Cynthia Shelhart
Liz Cifani
Wailing Banshees
Irish Fest Youth Choir

1993
Dordan with Mary Bergin
Eamonn McGirr
Kingston Trio
Four Men and a Dog
Suffering Gaels
Stack
Rawlins Cross
Tir na nóg
Fitz and the Celts
Donnybrook
Dave Gordon
Pagan Brothers
Leahy's Luck
Sean Og Mac Rachgan
The Riordans
Brigit's Fire

Music & Dancing

51

Stockton's Wing

Johnny McGreevy, Noel Rice, and Robert Gans

Eugene O'Donnell with Green Fields of America

Ann Conroy and Joe Burke

The Chieftains

Chip Deffaa doing tribute to
George M. Cohan

Tom Sweeney

Mary Ann Miller

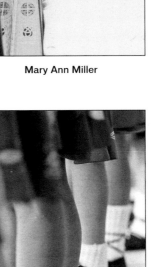

Asher Gray

Jeff Keeling, Gary Bottoni, Dan Hosmanek, Pat Williams, John Maher and Dennis Abere of Gael Wind

1994
Glenn Yarbrough
Brothers Four
Janet Harbison
Baltiorum
Sharon Shannon
Nightnoise
Hal Roach
The House Band
Finbar McCarthy
Kips Bay Ceili Band
Wolfstone
The Black Brothers
James Kelly Band
Ivers & Egan
Makem Brothers &
Brian Sullivan
180 and the Letter G
Folk Like Us

1995
Irish Descendants
Maire O'Keeffe
Aoife Clancy
Voice Squad
Clumsy Lovers
Black 47
Alias Ron Kavana
Brother
Paddy Noonan Band
Joe Burke, Amy McGann
& Felix Dolan
Blarney-20 Year Reunion
Maidin
Tempest
Loretto Reid &
Brian Taheny
Sigmund Snopek
McPeake Family

1996
Reeltime
The Irish Rovers
More Power to Your
Elbow
Moving Cloud
Solas
Bridget Fitzgerald
Joe Derrane
Wild Mountain Thyme
Martin Hayes & Dennis
Cahill
Robin Huw Bowen
Charlie Lennon
Roguery
Willowgreen

Music & Dancing

53

directors. The choir has given them confidence and helped them find their voices when sometimes they were very shy, she indicated. True to the Irish Fest connection, many have gone on to help other young people take up Irish instruments like the bodhran, fiddle and tin whistle and to become Irish Fest volunteers.

A deadly terrorist bombing in Omagh, Northern Ireland, on August 15, 1998, occurred during a festival weekend while Minister Sile de Valera of Ireland's Department of Arts, Heritage, Gaeltacht and the Islands, was on the grounds. The shock of that deadly horror impacted everyone at the festival that year. But the Omagh Community Youth Choir was born out of the tragedy.

That spirited choral group subsequently made its initial appearance at the festival in 2001 in a joint show with the Irish Fest Choir. Among the arrangements, the two groups of young people performed the uplifting hymn, *Across The Bridge of Hope*. When the song concluded, there was barely a dry eye in the audience. The talented young performers also visited the fest in 2003.

The fest promotes music with young people in other ways, as well. In the 1980s and 1990s, youngsters from the Milwaukee Junior Showcase regularly performed, spending countless hours learning Irish tunes for their presentation. A number of the performers went on to find other entertainment venues within the Irish Fest circle, such as Keith Moschea, who directed the play *Meg's Gold* in 1990.

This activity prompted a note to Ed Ward that same year from showcase coordinator Judy Stegeman (now Schwerm) pointing out that "the kids know that at Irish Fest, they are important, that they are trusted, and that the adults care about them. These qualities will only enhance them as adults.

Thank you, and the Irish Fest Board and directors, who over the years have brought not only a great festival to town, but also who have done so very much for the youth of our community."

Helping talent find its unique Irish voice is another festival tradition. Presentation of the annual Edward J. Ward Irish Music Scholarship has always been a festival highpoint, ever since the award was launched in 1989. Named in honor of festival founder Ward, the $1,000 grant aptly recognizes his ongoing efforts to promote Irish music and culture, as well as his community work.

Irish Fest's six-person entertainment committee meets regularly to consider bookings on the festival's main stages. The group consists of Ed Ward, Jane Anderson, Jane Walrath, Tom O'Connell, Barry Stapleton and Chuck Ward. As entertainment coordinator, Chuck Ward is also responsible for keeping everything moving along prior to and at the festival, plus working with sound staff, stagehands and volunteer stage crews during the event.

The entertainment committee meetings are often rambunctious affairs, with many names tossed around as the festival looks at different styles of bands. There are details to consider: whether the musicians have ever been in Milwaukee and were they well-received; are they particularly hot in Ireland, Canada and other venues; what do they cost; are they touring? It is also necessary to have a mix of male and female artists, as well as folk and traditional musicians. Since many fans come from states adjoining Wisconsin, the committee is interested in groups that can play year-round in the Midwest to build musical momentum for a festival appearance.

Committee representatives usually make a wish list, giving consideration to the acts that have been here in the recent

Liz Carroll

Barachois

Music & Dancing

Off Kilter

Joe Derrane

Tom Kennedy and Frank Patterson

Aoife Clancy

John Gary, Carmel Quinn and Joe Feeney

"Cuz" Teahan

1997
The Black
Family Reunion
Nomos
The Whole Shebang
Great Outdoors
Rock, Salt & Nails
Trian
Dermot Henry
Theiss & O'Connor
Stuart Martz Band
Curtis Crossroads Band
Heartstrings
The Rose and Dragon

1998
Natalie McMaster
Dervish
Clancy, O'Connell &
Clancy
The Makem Brothers
Old Blind Dogs
Ride
Green Fields of America
-20 Year Reunion
Tommy Sands
Chulrua
Nomos
Frogwater
Dubliner House Band
Paddy Keenan
Bridget Fitzgerald &
Gearóid Ó hAllmhuráin
Rira
The Kissers

1999
The New Barleycorn
La Bottine Souriante
Anam
Gaelic Storm
Donal Lunny & Coolfin
Seven Nations
Mary Custy Band
The Poor Clares
Anam Rí
Sean McGuire
Laurence Nugent Band
Celia Farran &
Brian Grinwald
Martin &
Christine Dowling
with Daithe Sproule
Tom Sweeney
John Williams &
Dean Magraw
Goat Crossing
Swallow's Tail Ceili Band
Canadian Celts
Jeff Ward
Gloria Hays
Bur
Free Whiski
Monica Marshall
Last Gaspe
Gabriel Hounds with
Brian McCoy
Standing Stones
Tom O' Sullivan
Last Night's Fun

Music & Dancing

55

past, others who have not been here for some time and bands that the fest reps have heard about but have not yet been in Milwaukee. Starting with a core of popular groups, the fest introduces new bands or new music concepts to keep the entertainment lineup fresh.

The entertainment committee books the main stages. Once an act is agreed upon and a tentative budget set, the committee members each take responsibility for contacting the artists or agents. As an example, Barry Stapleton handles the Rock Stage, with his choices confirmed by the committee. Coordinators who book the Harp, Gaeltacht, Children's Area, Crossroads, parades, theater and Summer School will work with the entertainment committee so everyone knows what performers are being considered.

If an act is available and contract terms agreeable, the committee moves ahead. Obviously, for every main act that is booked, some other acts need to be excluded. As acts are confirmed or determined not to be available, the committee again meets and goes through the process of discussing and picking replacements.

This booking concept works well since individual committee members have different musical interests and tastes. Some more actively follow developments on the Irish music scene and are more proactive in bringing in new ideas. "We certainly do not all agree on all bands and the discussion can be very animated but we always seem to come up with a resolution that is agreeable to a majority," said committee member Tom O'Connell.

The process is very different than it was in the early years when only a couple of individuals booked the acts. In those days, the young festival needed to go out and tell performers or their representatives what Irish Fest was all about. Now most of the artist representatives contact the festival with what they feel are hot CDs and press kits from their clients. The festival annually receives more than 600 inquiries about performing.

In the early years, as many of the bands were just becoming known, the Irish Fest organizers worked directly with the artists. As many of the performers grew more popular, it was increasingly necessary to deal with agents. This occasionally resulted in losing the personal touch with musicians who had become close friends of the event. Yet, some agents, such as the redoubtable Herschel Freeman who represents the Tannahill Weavers, retain that much-appreciated individual, hands-across-the-table business style. Freeman had also represented Irish Fest regulars like Natalie MacMaster, the "Golden Girl from Cape Breton," and La Bottine Souriante.

Freeman wrote a note to Ed Ward in 2000 after visiting Irish Fest. Praising the event, he said, "The great festivals create an environment both in the strength of the technical support system and the atmosphere on and off stage, that inspires the performers to reach beyond themselves for that ''special' performance."

Ward used to be able to listen to every recording sent in for review but the task is now impossible due to the volume of submissions. However, he still looks over each request that comes in, along with its accompanying materials. He then passes on the information to appropriate performance areas such as the Harp Tent or theater.

Mick Moloney

Danny Doyle

George Millar of the Irish Rovers

Daryl Simpson, Omagh Choir founder

Charlie Lennon

All materials that come in after a festival are kept in the archives and are accessible to the entertainment committee and anyone else who wants to go through the files. When materials are received, the office sends a notice from Chuck Ward acknowledging receipt and telling the sender that the festival will call them if interested in pursuing the act.

While many new ideas came from such unsolicited recordings in the past, most now come from artists who are on tour, Irish music commentators/writers or recommendations from other festival promoters. Fans of Irish Fest are also important and are encouraged to share their ideas with the festival. Unfortunately, due to the ever-tightening schedule, many bands cannot be invited to perform.

The music business is much more complicated today than it was 25 years ago. Today, there are numerous issues to consider: from finding new acts that create a festival buzz to ongoing wrestling with withholding taxes. Bands have more technical needs as they bring in or require more backline support. Some bands do not want to play all three days and contract fees keep rising. Visas and tax identification numbers are always an issue. There are also many challenges to bringing in bands from overseas. Among them are restrictive Homeland Security rules put in place after 9/11. Dealing with these types of complications falls under the purview of fest volunteer Attorney Pat Russell. Weather-related flight delays and musicians missing airline connections are other occasional headaches.

Over the years, the fest has broadened the entertainment mix to include various types of Celtic music. To some extent a band's popularity can be judged by its CD sales. Generally, new bands and new releases do well. Longtime volunteer and Blarney guitarist Dennis Murphy coordinates CD sales on the performers' behalf.

As part of this musical stretching, the fest has booked such bands as La Bottine Souriante (Quebec) and Barachois (Prince Edward Island). While not Irish, they have a strong Celtic flavor. Many forms of American popular and folk music have been profoundly influenced by Irish and Irish American musicians, dancers and composers since

2000
Clancy Family Reunion
Great Big Sea
The Prodigals
The Bumblebees
Sliabh Notes
Off Kilter
Sean McGuire &
Joe Burke
Brian Conway &
Mark Simos
Eugene Byrne
The Elders
Lunasa
Brigid's Cross
Different Drums of Ireland
Fintan Vallely &
Charlie Piggott
Marie Ni Chathasaigh &
Chris Newman
Saw Doctors
Danu
Liz Carroll
Sullivan Brothers
Pat Woods
Castle Band
Kathy Cowan
Barry Dodd

2001
Beginish
Barleycorn Reunion
Barachois
Eileen Ivers Band
Dara
Four Courts Ceili Band
Bohola
The Fenians
Rinka
Melanie O'Reilly
Glencastle Irish Dancers
Celia Farran
John Whelan Band
Kissers
Daryl Simpson
Paddy Glackin &
Robbie Hannan
Omagh Youth Choir
Derek McCormack

2002
The Highwaymen
North Cregg
Brendan Nolan
Kim Robertson
Shooglenifty
Kila
The Commitments
Tracy Sands Band
3 Pints Gone
Sean Tyrell
Seamus Connolly
Brendan Bulger &
Jim de Wan
Evans & Doherty
Kilfenora Ceili Band
Spain Brothers
Clumsy Lovers
Tom O'Carroll
David HB Drake
Providence
Bohola
Leahy
Fiona Molloy
Siucra

Different Drums' Stephen Matier

Dermot Henry

America's early history. Subsequently, the fest promises to continue making a concerted effort going forward to educate people about the cross-fertilization of Irish and American musical forms over the past 200 years. A new Celtic Roots Tent was introduced in 2005 to celebrate many of these musical themes.

It is all a far cry from 1981 when the festival offered only four entertainment stages. Three were brewery-labeled: Schlitz, Miller and Pabst. The fourth was the Children's Stage. Roaming musicians fleshed out the sound, so that every corner of the festival seemed filled with lilting song by dozens of groups over the years, including Sungarden, Northern Lights, Gretta Comiskey & Lorraine Murphy, Malcolm the Wanderer, Samhradh and St. James's Gate. Even such powerhouses as all-Ireland piper Paul Deloughery, performing with Anna Grinwald and Michele McNulty of the Cashel Academy of Irish Dance, made appearances.

Folk singer David H.B. Drake has been a fest fixture around the grounds since the beginning, usually appearing as Carrie O'Tunne.

For these street musicians, there have been challenges: walking and singing for eight to 10 hours straight for three days, plus performing stage sets. Heat, rain, bugs, staying in tune and raw fingers are part of the job. "But, I wouldn't trade it for the world," Drake affirmed.

There has always been plenty of room to grow and improvise at Irish Fest. The Rock Stage originally started as a teen tent with taped music, organized by young supervisors such as Dan Hintz, Mike Walrath and a contingent of others whose parents worked at the festival. The idea was to give the young people something they could relate to and enjoy, a factor which eventually led to putting together a major stage presence for the more "hip" and "trendy" bands.

Bagpipers lend another fun element to the parades through the grounds

Sean McGuire, Mick Moloney and Joe Burke

Glen Yarbrough and his daughter Holly

O'Connell Sisters, Milwaukee Junior Showcase, 1981

Although there were a number of people in the organization in 1988 and 1989 who did not think this theme fit into the festival or were worried that it would negatively change the "feel" of the event, the Rock Stage has become one of the most popular areas and attracts huge crowds of all ages. The festival management listened to all these comments and decided to utilize a stage on the North End where the sound would have minimal impact on the rest of the festival.

As such, by 2004, 16 performance areas were being utilized, with more than 100 groups spread over the grounds and presenting more than 200 individual performances. The festival attempts to give musicians good slots and tries not to pit groups against each other more than

once during the weekend. Although some performers gripe about being on smaller stages, some love it, Chuck Ward emphasized. Most bands, however, are simply happy to be at Milwaukee Irish Fest.

Assigning acts to stages is a delicate and often worrisome process, explained Chuck Ward, who said, "Every band must be given an opportunity to 'show its stuff.'" Well-known bands get the best stage slots but since the festival has five major stages, it must be careful not to book a lesser-known band the same time every day against a better-known band. "We try to have different music styles on at all times so we don't have people saying that the music 'all sounds the same,'" according to Ward. "We must also consider the food and retail vendors in each

Irish Rovers

2003
Slainte Mhath
Flook
Makem & Spain Brothers
Cottars
Eidir
Jarvies
Green Side Up
David Kincaid
Daragh de Bruin Band
Waking Maggie
Barra MacNeills
Seamus Kennedy
Linda Rutherford & Celtic Fire
Carbon Leaf
Afro Celts
Salt Creek
Jeremy Kittel
Brendan Nolan
Charlie Piggott & John Egan
Kissers
Tommy Peoples
Switchback
Errigal

2004
Teada
Tommy Fleming
Pipeline
The Wise Maids
Bad Haggis with Eric Rigler
Ragus
McKrells
James Kelly & Daithi Sproule
St. Brendan's Voyage
The Kells
All Set Ceili Band
Furey Brothers
Ce
Luka Bloom

2005
The Bridies
Garrison Brothers
Young Dubliners
Kinsella Irish Dancers
Bruce Molsky
Bob Pasch as Bing Crosby
Chip Deffaa as George M. Cohan
Barley Bree Reunion
Blarney 30th Anniversary
McComiskey, Mulvihill & McLeod
Tynkyr Boys
Hothouse Flowers
U2Zoo
Liz Caroll & John Doyle
Salt Creek
O'Shyttes
Gan Bua
Chicago All Stars
Reilly
McMenamin Irish Dance Academy

Music & Dancing

59

Steve Wehmeyer of Gaelic Storm

James Kelly, Dolores Keane, John Faulkner and Jackie Daly of Kinvara

Joe Derrane and John Whalen

area and balance the stages so that no one area gets all the hot acts and resultant crowds."

Among the reasons that the festival is appreciated is the fact that new bands can be exposed to the many other Irish-festival directors who attend from around North America. Playing at Milwaukee can be a plus for bands that wisely promote their appearances at the fest, contributing to their eventual success. For instance, the fest was the first major event to book Gaelic Storm, the sit-up-and-take-notice band from the award-winning film *Titanic*. "We took a chance and so did they. It ended up being a win-win for both of us," agreed Ed Ward.

Local and regional groups can also be noticed by outsiders. Seán Laffey, of Dublin-based *Irish Music Magazine*, told his readers in 2001 to "keep an eye out" for Milwaukee-based Anam Ri, led by Asher Gray on flute, whistles and bouzouki. "They are a fine traditional four-piece that can on occasion step beyond the line and rack up some very exciting experimental music." Anam Ri was subsequently featured in the magazine's "Up and Coming" section.

Irish Fest has also helped many musicians involved in the local Irish music scene. As a result, there are numerous quality bands available to perform in the city's Irish pubs and other venues each weekend and particularly on the High Holy Holidays surrounding St. Patrick's Day.

Yet occasionally everything does not work out exactly as planned. In 2001, Luka Bloom was unable to do his show due to last-minute problems with the United States Immigration and Naturalization Service regarding his performer's visa. Nevertheless, the classy Melanie O'Reilly was quickly drafted as last-minute replacement and, of course, sang magnificently. In the same year, uilleann piper Robbie Hannan was rushed to a local hospital for an emergency appendectomy, which prevented him from performing a highly anticipated show with Paddy Glackin, the original fiddler with the renowned Bothy Band. Most bookings do eventually work out, with Bloom finally making it to the festival in 2004.

Contributing to the success of the fest and the musicians' enthusiastic feelings about the event are the hardworking stage managers and their crews who tend to the entertainers' needs. Kevin and Dan Costello, along with Joe King, have managed the Old Style Stage since 1985. They've worked with such stars as Frank Patterson, The Irish Rovers, Leahy, Paddy Reilly, The Chieftains, Carmel Quinn, Eileen Ivers, Gaelic Storm, Donal Lunny and Coolfin and De Danann.

Typical of all the stages, the managers arrive early on the Friday morning of the festival for daylong sound checks coordinated by professionals such as Eric West, the Old Style house man since the early 2000s. During the sound check, the crew reacquaints itself with the familiar acts and greets the new groups. During the festival, the stage managers get the bands on and off in quick rotation, making timeliness another festival hallmark. After the fest, all the stage managers meet to talk about the good and the bad and to give their takes on the performers.

Vince Shiely has been an Irish Fest stage manager ever since Day One. Aided by Brad Krebs and Tim Benson, Shiely took over the Miller Stage from Rick Erickson in the early 1980s and has been there since then. With all that experience, the operation seems to proceed almost on autopilot, but every year more tweaking is done to make it even smoother. The proximity of the stage to the audience and its intimacy has made it a favorite for the likes of Tommy Makem, Gaelic Storm, Barley Bree, Schooner Fare and others who have become first-name friends with Shiely.

Performers know they can rely on us to take care of their needs, and we take that trust very seriously," emphasized Jim O'Keeffe, another two-decade festival veteran who handles the scene on the Aer Lingus Stage. "Without that, there is no respect. And we need respect and trust to keep the stage running on time," he said. O'Keeffe knows the music scene from all sides, by performing as a guitar soloist and with the old Minstrel Druids, a group he formed in the early 1980s.

For the stage managers, Irish Fest continues to be an action-packed, basically sleepless weekend where one has to constantly be on top of things and check blood pressure and heart rate, laughed O'Keeffe and the other stage managers. Keeping everyone happy, though, is probably the most challenging aspect of stage managing, they each assert. "But that is also the most fun part as well," indicated O'Keeffe, who added that a good sense of humor was not only necessary in the job description, it was essential. O'Keeffe works the Aer Lingus Stage with his brother, Mike, and nephew, Joe, along with life-time friend Paul (Tall Paul) Jablonski.

There is always a pall cast over the festival crew when it is learned that a performer friend has died, sometimes suddenly. Among those who have gone on to the Great

Natalie McMaster

African drummers and dancers join local Irish dancers

Scattering have been fiddler Sean McGuire; Ralph Garrett, Tommy Makem's long-time agent; singer Frank Patterson; Tom Rowe of Schooner Fare; Derek Bell, harpist with the Chieftains; Jimmy Ferguson of the Irish Rovers; Derek McCormack of Barleycorn; Frank Harte; John Byrne; and Tommy Makem's wife, Mary; Paddy Clancy, Bobby Clancy and Tom Clancy, among others. When possible, festival representatives have attended funerals of their entertainer colleagues.

The festival takes great pains to care for the performers once they are booked, including assisting with visas and arranging accommodations. Irish Fest consideration has been demonstrated in many small ways. In the early days, female artists were pleasantly surprised to have roses in their hotel rooms upon check-in.

It is particularly important to be sure that rooms are available for the musicians and their entourages. Jeanne Cissne, Volunteer of the Year for 2004, acts as unofficial den leader for the entertainers in her capacity as accommodations director. In 1992, while still organizing the festival's Thursday evening kickoff, Cissne received her current assignment keeping track of the six facilities where performers are lodged. Another title for her might be "House Mother to the Stars."

In this capacity, Cissne sees little of what is happening on the grounds. Instead, she lives at the Park East, the festival's hotel headquarters, and experiences life behind the scenes. Cissne stays at the hotel from the Wednesday before the festival through the following Monday, holding court at a desk in the Park East lobby near the main desk. Performers and teachers for the Summer School may start arriving a week early and there is always plenty to do during checkout when the fest closes.

Among Cissne's responsibilities are booking accommodations for 30 or more groups that perform at the fest. In addition, she works closely with Tom and Julie Smith, who head the festival's transportation staff. The trio coordinates arrivals and departures and arranges shuttles to and from the Park East Hotel and the grounds for performances.

Legendary parties at the Park East have long been part of Irish Fest lore, with performers holding impromptu jam sessions from the hotel's basement to its rooftop and attending much-talked-about parties in the basement hosted by the late Michael Clarke. The band Gaelic Storm has always given high praise to the Park East and even wrote a song, now recorded on one of their CDs, about what happens at the caravansary when the Irish arrive.

Some performers are also hosted in the Shorewood neighborhood surrounding the home of Phil and Mary June Hanrahan, who for years have arranged many musicians' accommodations with their friends. There is always time for a party at the Hanrahans, as well. In 1994, the house was packed with visiting entertainers, including fiddler James Kelly, arranger/producer Zan McLeod, tin whistle impresario

It's usually a full house in the Dance Tent

Bridget O' Sullivan, Asher Gray and Evan Leahy of Anam Ri

Greenfields of America featuring stepdancers Donny Golden and Michael Flatley, 1981

Leahy's Luck

Mary Bergin and still more. On the late afternoon of that festival's Thursday, the kettle was boiling, chairs were dragged into the kitchen and sandwiches thrown together for a last bite before going down to the grounds for the night.

Some volunteers, however, don't have such regular contact with the performers and are unable to take in many of the shows. But they are not neglected. The bank has a standing rule that when a performer comes in to cash a check, they are requested to sing or play their instrument. The request is usually met with the approval of the entertainers who feel sorry for locked-away number-crunchers.

For accountant/musician Kristina Paris who volunteers in the bank, accuracy and timeliness are all-important. Prior to the festival, she ensures that the contracts are properly signed and that all the entertainers have filled in the mandatory information.

The system continues to improve since returning musicians have all the paperwork in order and the database gets more and more complete. Also, since the bank area is so small and Paris is not the only one using the computer to print checks, bank crewmembers must carefully coordinate the timing of their tasks. Paris also needs to make sure all the checks get to the entertainers' stages during their last performances.

Dance has always been an integral component of Milwaukee Irish Fest, an activity popular long before touring shows captured the public's imagination. Donny, Barbara and Eileen Golden were regulars with the early Green Fields of America. Michael Flatley, soon to be of *Riverdance* and *Lord of the Dance* fame, also performed at Irish Fest. He danced as a teenager in the early 1980s and wowed the crowd with his jumps and athleticism.

The Walsh and the Geary Irish dancers performed alongside Gael Wind in the early 1980s. Matt O'Maoileidigh and his champion troupe were a hit at the 1990 Summer School. The fabled Jean Butler of *Riverdance* was one of the primary instructors at the school in 2003 and 2004, returning to teach and perform in 2005.

When Irish Fest started in 1981, a general policy was that artists or dancers who were actively a part of the local Irish music and dance scene would always have a place there. The fest has followed this rule to the fullest extent possible, knowing that this opportunity to perform will give musicians and dancers a wonderful showcase. It is one which will in turn promote more musicians and dancers.

This is exactly what has happened. In the dance area, for example, when Irish Fest started there was one dance school with 30-plus dancers. With the 25th festival, there were five dance schools with more than 4,000 dancers in the Milwaukee area. Following in the rhythmic steps of the Trinity Academy of

Irish Dance and Cashel-Dennehy School of Irish Dance are the Glencastle Irish Dancers, the Kinsella Academy of Irish Dance and the McMenamin Irish Dance Academy.

This presents the event with a major, but marvelous, challenge of trying to work in all the acts. Attempting to treat all the dance schools fairly in terms of number of shows and stage assignments may soon require the wisdom of a McSolomon.

These productions by the young performers in each troupe have often sparkled with amazing moments. For several years, Trinity performed a dance collaboration with a contingent of African American dancers from Milwaukee. World champion Becky Cissne Slaske recalled that she was lucky enough to be included in these performances, usually done at the end of Trinity's show on the Old Style Stage.

"As soon as the dance was done, we held our final position with the African dancers. I remember the crowd jumping up and screaming. There were people in the front rows crying at what they saw. The audience got it! The two very different cultures coming together and creating such a beautiful piece of art. It was amazing," she exclaimed.

Leahy

So, while there are many more acts out there now and Irish music is more mainstream today, the festival is held to a much higher entertainment standard than in the past because of its well-earned reputation.

Everyone has their own memorable moments when it comes to the festival's musical presentations. Among them could be counted:

 Tom Paxton, Schooner Fare and the Limeliters performing together on the Leinie's Rock Stage during the U.S. Steel Great American Hootenanny revival in 1992. Their singing of *Let There Be Peace on Earth* was as close to being back in the 1960s as anyone could imagine as the crowd sang along and waved lights.

The Scattering brings performers together for a grand festival finale

James McNally and Tommy McMenamin of Storm had the crowd really going one year. At the completion of one song, McMenamin rose from his chair while holding his banjo, which he proceeded to smash on the stage as the crowd roared. Ed Ward kept the banjo head, had each musician autograph it and then placed the piece in the festival's archives.

 The 1987 Flood Year in which rain, wind and lightning meant moving many of the acts to the Marcus Amphitheater on the South End of the grounds.

Gaelic Storm meets fans

After one of his early visits to Milwaukee, musician/historian Mick Moloney said, "We all travel to several festivals each year and I personally have been in the course of the last 10 years to every major festival in America. I can say, categorically, that yours is the finest both in the caliber of performers chosen and also in the warmth and hospitality which is extended to the performers." He then went on to enthusiastically compliment Irish Fest for the professionalism of its general operations behind the scenes. Coming as it did from such a respected entertainer, this was praise from on high, indeed.

When all was said and done, Irish music journalist/historian Fintan Valley "took a chair-lift across the vast campus of the annual Irish Fest of music and culture in Milwaukee, and spied plenty of gold among the shamrocks," reported *The Irish Times* of September 4, 1997.

For anyone on an Irish musical quest, who could ask for more?

Paddy Glackin and John Doyle

La Bottine Souriante

Cherish the Ladies

Chapter 5

Eamonn O'Neill and Dermod Lynskey

Celtic Treasures

Culture

Celtic Treasures

Culture

The Cultural Area -- or more officially, Ballyfest Cultural Village -- of Milwaukee Irish Fest is clearly a "festival within a festival." Many patrons who come to the festival spend an entire day or more in this area. The size and scope of the offerings clearly distinguish Irish Fest from other ethnic and Celtic festivals. The area -- supervised by board member Tadhg McInerney, who is helped by project coordinators -- grew from a small stage to eventually encompass the entire South End of the grounds.

The area includes a theater, pub, genealogy and harp tents, the Moore Street Marketplace, archives and cultural tents, Hedge School, Gaeltacht, currach area and Literary Corner. This area is a perfect example of Irish Fest's personal and cultural growth over the years and its consistent efforts to try to incorporate all aspects of Irish culture into the event format.

Such exhibits are important because some of the first Irish performers at the festival noted the misconceptions that Americans had about Irish culture in general. They emphasized that Irishness was not just about leprechauns and shamrocks, but something far deeper and much richer. Subsequently, the festival's mission has long been to banish those outdated notions. The heavy menu of cultural surprises, for those who take the time to meander the exhibits and take in the lectures, appears to be working. Irish Fest friends, such as Dublin-born John Gleeson, promoted Milwaukee and Irish Fest in their native country. Gleeson was an important cultural conduit for the festival to and from Ireland in the 1980s and through the early 1990s.

There is an interesting twist. Among the best compliments received over the past 15 years by cultural exhibits co-coordinator Brian Witt is that the native Irish now coming to Milwaukee say they have learned more about their country's culture, history or music than they did at home.

Delighted with her stay, the range of cultural offerings and the new friends she met, "I told everyone and anyone about it (the festival) and showed my photos to them," enthused Christine Sawyer, a quilter from Cape Clear Island, Cork, who demonstrated her craft in 2004.

Hundreds of displays have been erected throughout Irish Fest's 25 years, including an award-winning 16-panel exhibit in 1984 from the Guinness Brewery Museum, featuring James Joyce memorabilia and photos. Special appearances by craftworkers, such as Irish crystal cutter Paddy Flaherty demonstrating his art in 1991, heighten the area's appeal. Broad themes are important, too. In 2004, the cultural area focused on the wondrous islands of Ireland. Relating offshore legends and lore were Mícheál de Mordha from the Great Blasket Island Center in Dunquin, Co. Kerry, and Mairead O'Reilly, director of the Irish Island Federation.

In 2005, the Cultural Village was swept up in the anniversary celebration, with the art of crystal cutting in the Waterford Shop being a major attraction. The company even donated a large chandelier to the festival, presenting the gift during the opening hooley night program. Other displays included the history of Irish circuses and an exhibit of long-time volunteer Bob Burke's presenting a fabulous view of the Irish in "Paddy Postcards in Caricature." Irish weaver Beth Moran and knitter Maire O'Flatharta demonstrated their skills.

Postcards could be purchased at the Irish Fest Stores and sent from the Cultural Village, stamped with a special 25th anniversary United States mail postmark.

The first cultural coordinator was Tom Cannon, at the time a professor at the Marquette University Law School, who had heard about plans for the festival in the summer of 1980. He met with his sister, Mary Cannon, and with Ed and

Chuck Ward to discuss organizing a cultural component for that initial event. "Ed Ward told us his idea for an Irish Fest, one that would be an emerald version of Festa Italiana. From that meeting, an Irish Fest Coordinating Committee developed, with supervisors in such areas as music, food, tickets, volunteers, publicity, fundraising and culture," recalled Cannon. He volunteered to head up the cultural tent because of his long-standing interest in Irish history and genealogy. Cannon wanted to see that this aspect of Irish culture was done correctly and presented well. He also wanted to steer the discussion of Irish history away from a negative focus of being a victim of British imperialism and towards a positive look at the many riches of Irish culture.

While participating in the first fest, Cannon admitted being surprised at the range of traditional Irish music being offered. He had suffered through an earlier lifetime of hearing only saccharine ballads like "Danny Boy" and "Mother Machree" or pub songs and "McNamara's Band."

"I absolutely fell in love with the music created by Mick Moloney's Green Fields of America. I bought their album and have been listening to it ever since. Over the years I have collected more than a hundred albums of traditional Irish music," Cannon added.

As the initial coordinator of the cultural tent, he then spent most of his volunteer time researching potential exhibits and contacting museums and other outlets to request loans and confirm permissions. For those first displays, he worked with Peter Brown, librarian at Trinity College, Dublin; David Born, curator of the Smart Museum at the University of Chicago; Harry Anderson, executive director of the Milwaukee County Historical Society; Mary O'Reilly, cultural relations chair of the Irish American Heritage Center in Chicago; the Catholic University Press; the old Irish Tourist Board; and the State Historical Society of Wisconsin.

Among the displays was a collection of color photos of Ireland taken by Bob Higgins, the legendary chronicler of the city's Irish community in the 1960s and 1970s. In addition, festgoers enjoyed a series of 16 full-size reproductions from the 7th century *Book of Darrow*; replicas of prehistoric and medieval art treasures that had originally been presented at the 1893 Chicago World's Fair and maps showing the pattern of Irish settlement in Wisconsin. Sarah Brown Dann and Mary Ellen Simet loaned Irish craftwork including Connemara marblework, Belleek china and Celtic jewelry from their shop, Erin Ltd.

After that hectic first year, it was obvious that a broader committee was needed to pull the the cultural area together. Cannon was followed by Dr. Nancy Walczyk who started as coordinator in 1982. She is currently associate director of the University of Wisconsin-Milwaukee's Center for Celtic Studies and a fluent Gaelic speaker. She had heard about the festival from John Maher at a meeting in the home of Gareth and Janet Dunleavy and also at the Shamrock Club meetings when Ed Ward outlined the festival plans. The late Dunleavys, on the English faculty at the University of Wisconsin-Milwaukee, were highly regarded Irish scholars who regularly visited Ireland to research and write. They became helpful in suggesting and planning some of the initial cultural presentations.

Walcyzk first volunteered to work in the information booths. Having a great time and loving the music, she then agreed to take over the cultural area for 1982 when asked by Cannon and Ward.

Walczyk brought in the University of Wisconsin-Milwaukee folk harp group to put together a program to play in the cultural tent in the early 1980s, a factor which helped popularize interest in that musical genre. Several harpists such as Patrick Ball, Angus Fallon MacGregor and Mary Ann Miller, were also popular on the old Folk Stage. That site morphed

In the harp tent

Nancy Madden Walczyk

Dave O'Meara

Culture

into a Folk-Harp Stage in 1987. In 1988, in addition to managing the cultural area, Walczyk launched a full-blown Harp Tent to accommodate the discerning tastes of festgoers.

That first year set the tone for ensuing harp programs. The Milwaukee Folk Harp Ensemble participated in a concert with an accompanying lecture, featuring the life and music of Turlough O'Carolan, the famed 17th century Irish harpist. Jeanne Henderson, Gerry Elliott, Lisa Ibarra, Crystal Woolsey, Jeanne Kahn and Carol Meves, and Lynn Michel rounded out the offerings with their rich, vibrant melodies.

The Harp Tent, under the direction of Dorothy Walsh, is now an integral part of the festival's overall package and showcases a wide range of international, regional and local talent. Often, the harp music is augmented by cello or flute and poetry and vocals. Janet Harbison, Kim Robertson, Aislinn and Megahn Gagliardi, Sue Richards, Rick Stanley, Cindy Shelhart, Maire ni Chathasaigh and dozens more have appeared over the years. In 2005, the fest hosted Irish harpers Una Flhannagain and Michelle Mulcahy, among its strong lineup of performers.

Ohio-native Ann Comer moved to Milwaukee in 1983 to practice law and became involved in Irish Fest that year after being recruited by John Maher. "He asked if I would like to volunteer for a few hours at the festival and invited me to an board meeting where he introduced me as the new gate coordinator. This was unbeknownst to me, a position that required me to be at the Irish Fest grounds full time, rather than for just a few hours," Comer recalled with a smile. That job extended from 1983 to 1986.

When Irish Fest established the area supervisor structure in 1986, Comer was then appointed one of the first four area supervisors. Two were appointed from the board and two were non-board members, one of whom was Comer. Until 1993, she supervised the Cultural Area and Cultural Village;

and Grafton Square retail; Liturgy; Athletics; Services; Parade; Information; Posters; and Clan Reunions.

When Comer became supervisor for the Cultural Area, the site was located in one tent not far from what is now the Irish Fest office, which is just south of the center of the grounds. In that tent were harp and theater performances and the cultural displays. Gleeson, Walczyk and Comer wanted to move the Cultural Area into a village setting. So about 1986, Comer went to the board and asked for a budget that would allow them to move the area to the far south end of the grounds and create a "town."

Comer also became busy with Irish Fest management, serving two terms on the board of directors and becoming its secretary. She was then board vice president in 1992 and president of the festival in 1993. Following these jobs, she coordinated the Irish Fest Bank in 1994, organized the first visit of the Spirit of Galway to the festival in 1995 and has acted as tour coordinator since then. Comer has also been a member of the Irish Fest Foundation board of directors since it was established in 1994.

Up until the mid-1990s, the Cultural Area was coordinated by Comer, Gleeson and Walczyk, with Gleeson and Walczyk doing the exhibits and artistic arrangments, while Comer handled the operational part of the job and setup. In 1993, the Irish Fest Village became an area all its own, with its own supervisor. Coordinators were appointed for each tent. Mary Otto became the area supervisor in 1993 and served in that capacity until her death. Under her, the village and its popularity expanded and the Moore Street Market was added. Murphy's Pub, managed by Mike Brady, is a comfortable place in the Cultural Area to put up one's feet, have a pint and listen to the likes of such marvelous musicians as Tommy Keane & Jacqueline McCarthy, Barry Dodd, Jeff Ward and Sean McRactagan and to be swept away by the wonderful Welsh singing of Geraint Wilkes.

Ann Kerns Comer

Dorothy Walsh

John Gleeson

Culture

69

Wendy Landvatter and Brian Witt

Ray Mac Mánais

The next cultural display coordinator was Kathy Radaj who had long been active with the Shamrock Club. In 1988, Radaj took over as solo coordinator for the tent, since Walczyk wanted to concentrate on the Hedge School. In those early 1980s, after that first big splashy year, there was no money to pay for visiting craftsmen from Ireland or laminated exhibits, Radaj recalled. So the cultural area workers used colored construction paper and photocopies from books they owned or had borrowed from the library to make up the exhibits. One year, they paid $12.95 and waited two weeks for reproductions of four photos from the Milwaukee Historical Society for an exhibit on the Old Third Ward Fire, she said.

Walczyk asked Radaj to join her officially as a coordinator of the Cultural Tent about the time they started running out of new crafts to showcase. But, with John Gleeson as the idea man, the group formulated a cultural theme/focus for the year and a plan of action was launched. "John's ideas and schemes were sometimes outlandish, but always creative and authentically Irish, plus we had John to put the Irish imprimatur on it," Radaj said.

Out-of-town guests were put up in local homes to save on hotel costs and presentations were often paid for by the Shamrock Club or the Ancient Order of Hibernians, two organizations that have always been generous Cultural Area sponsors. "So, my job evolved into that of Lord High Executioner of Plans as Brian Witt, Bob Hamill and Ed Mikush joined our team with Ann Comer and then Mary Otto, our wonderful area supervisors, running interference and promoting our corner of the festival with the Irish Fest board," Radaj indicated.

She was particularly proud of the part she played in helping develop and arrange for such exhibits as the St. Brigit's Holy Well, Tory Island artists, a major Guinness display, the Hall of Presidents of Irish Heritage and the Press Photographers Association of Ireland Photos of the Year, among many others.

Witt became a valuable member of the team, being Shamrock Club president from 1995 to 1996 after being vice president and a trustee. Witt was also an incorporating board member of the Irish Cultural and Heritage Center. With a lifelong love of Irish music and theater, Witt's Irish career also included being a

The St. Barbara, a replica of a sailboat called a "Galway hooker," visits Irish Fest

concert promoter, broadcaster and playwright, as well as acting as webmaster for several Celtic associations.

Typical of many Irish Fest volunteers, he began helping in 1981 and served in several capacities. He eventually wound up in the cultural area, aiding Kathy Radaj and Nancy Walczyk from 1986 to 1988. In 1991, Witt was appointed co-coordinator with Radaj. In 2002, Radaj moved over full time to the Theatre Tent and Witt took over the Culture Tent on his own. In 2002, Cynthia Nazario began volunteering and Sonya Cunningham joined the team the following year. Both are now Witt's assistant coordinators.

Witt is usually on the grounds all week, from the Saturday prior to the Monday after the fest. As with the other hardworking veterans, he is afraid to add up the hours put in by all the volunteers. In the early 2000s, the grounds setup group was divided in half because the entire Cultural Area took almost as many hours to set up as did the rest of the festival. This is in part because of the area's quirky nature and the number of individual exhibits and attractions, such as the High Cross, the Ogham stone, the sacred well and other displays. Setup involves determining sight lines, traffic patterns and a general sense of "this isn't working like this" causing the coordinators to move displays at the last minute.

Bob Hamill heads the operations crew for the South End, a task further subdivided to Joe Hughes for some tents, Ed Mikush for the painting and many others. This ensures efficiency, with the team aiming for a Thursday completion because Fridays at the festival are pressure-cooker days. It now helps that Witt knows ahead of time that certain workers will be performing specific jobs, rather than relying on earnest drop-bys.

Bui Bolg puppets from Co. Waterford

Others in the diverse cultural crew include the Murphys of Milwaukee and St. Louis: Dan, Dave and Mary, one an electrician, the other a pediatric doctor in the critical-care area of a St. Louis hospital, and Herself a retired nurse. Tom Tibbals, a truck driver, Pat Fitzgibbons, a cattle buyer in the real world, and all sorts of other folks take vacation time or a break from their retirements to do grunt work for a week. They have a sense of ownership in the area and a sense of pride seeing it come together.

The biggest challenge for the Cultural Area is to remain fresh, using displays for no more than two years in a row. Longtime visitors look for the new exhibits and want to be educated, entertained and wowed.

Tadhg McInerney works throughout the year when it comes to budgets. He first meets with his coordinators to review financial plans and then incorporates the entire cultural group: harp, genealogy, theater, archives, Gaeltacht, pub, Waltons, Hedge School, currachs, hurlers, Moore Street Market and Literary Corner. The Irish Fest Summer School, a week of classes preceding the festival, is also represented because the instructors can perform or lecture in the Gaeltacht, the Harp Tent, the Theater, the Cultural Tent and with Genealogy to share overall costs.

Mrs. Sean O'Casey

The exhibits are discussed with festival director Jane Anderson. Then Nazario, Cunningham and Witt plan their exhibits and consider their participants. Anderson subsequently seeks sponsorship to cover plane fare and housing. There are always last-minute additions, a factor not fazing the organizers who are well-used to the shuffling.

Culture

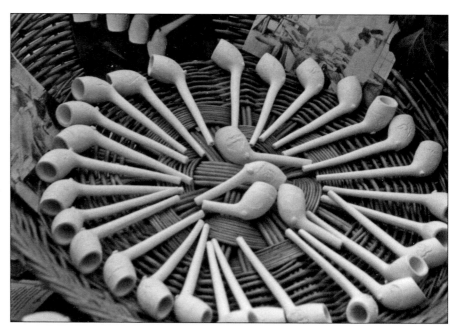

Clive O'Keefe uses branches and sticks to
build a replica of an early currach

Ethel Kelly's clay pipes

Assembling the details is a study in organization because
authenticity is all-important. The festival, aided with funds
from the Ancient Order of Hibernians and Shamrock Club of
Wisconsin, employed Milwaukee Repertory Theater set
builder Paul Gegenhuber to construct a High Cross for the
center of the Cultural Village. The towering structure and its
plaque, symbolizing the motivation of the Cultural Area
volunteers, is a reproduction of the original Cross of the
Scriptures at Clonmacnois. Its dedication in 1990 was a real
watershed for Kathy Radaj, who helped coordinate its
building, based on an idea of John Gleeson. In that year, she
was also honored as the Irish Rose for 1990 by the Shamrock
Club, and Ed Ward was honored as Irishman of the Year.

A ton of sandstone rocks was purchased another year to
demonstrate construction of stone walls. The next year, the
Cultural Tent coordinators implored Summerfest officials to let
them use limestone from along the lake walk, which they did.

In yet another display, a currach was built by Peter Mulkerrin,
a Connemara resident of Pittsburgh. A willow corracle, a
small round boat, was made by Cliabh O Guibhne (Clive
O'Givney), a native of the Boyne River Valley in Ireland. A
functioning still -- used by Bartley O'Dohmnaill from
Connemara to demonstrate distillation of poteen, that
headsplitting bootleg whiskey -- was built in Chicago by
Steve Mulkerrins, another Connemara émigré. Mulkerrins also
constructed the St. Barbara, a Galway hooker that became a

Waltons Bodhran Summer School

Graine O'Maithu

hit with the sailing set at the 2004 festival. Yes, Mulkerrin and Mulkerrins are different families.

In 1997, the rain poured down and flooded the South End because the reeds O Guibhne used to make his corracle plugged one of the drains, causing the overflow. But when the water was deep enough, he gave boat rides inside the tent to delighted exhibitors. Amid the rush of water, O'Dohmnaill distributed whiskey to everyone and the wife of an Irish governmental official even asked if she might have a "wee dram." 'Twas just another grand ol' time at Irish Fest.

Speaking of boats, a replica of a hold from one of the notorious "coffin" ships that transported thousands of Irish to America during the Famine was displayed in 1995 and 1996. The exhibit was built by the festival's workers under the direction of Bob Hamill. The exhibit was based on one at the Ulster American Folk Park in Omagh, Northern Ireland.

The festival's workers also demonstrated their skills in constructing a craft in 2002, modeled on one used in the 6th century by fabled Irish adventurer St. Brendan. Dimensions of the boat were taken from a book entitled *The Brendan Voyage* by author Tim Severin, who built and sailed a currach similar to those used by Irish monks to traverse the Atlantic. The workers used some of the wood from the famine ship display to build the currach. Other exhibits have also been recycled and redone, such as the Hall of American Presidents which became a Limerick Station train display.

For the most part, Cultural Area exhibitors are impressed with the entire setup, which is like a mystical Brigadoon as it appears and disappears each year, as the late Mary Otto once pointed out. Before the demonstrators arrive, many are uncertain of what the grounds are like and so the vastness of the festival sometimes overwhelms them once they enter the grounds. Occasionally, the visitors are "lost" to the wonders of the overall festival for a day or so. But they do eventually return to their proper spot or are retrieved by hunter/handlers from the Cultural Area.

Mary Clancy, widow of famed musician Paddy Clancy, was impressed with a 1999 display featuring her husband's works. The renowned musician had died the preceding November. "I could never have imagined just how huge the festival is," she wrote in a note after her visit. "I really had to be there. So

many times, Paddy told me about it and I appreciated the pleasure and enjoyment he got from being there...now my heart has a rich glow which has come from all the warmth and outpouring of love I have brought home with me from your wonderful festival."

While in Milwaukee, Clancy announced the establishment of the Paddy Clancy Memorial Scholarship Fund, which received a $2,500 financial kickstart from the Irish Fest Foundation. She also visited the John J. Ward, Jr., Irish Music Archives at the Irish Fest Center to donate some of Paddy's memorabilia. The gift included more than 50 valuable recordings from the Tradition Label, which was started by Paddy Clancy in 1955. These discs from Clancy's own collection include many Irish artists, including the first Clancy Brothers & Tommy Makem records along with other legendary performers such as the fabled blues and folk musician Odetta and singer/songwriter Ewan McColl.

Irish actor Dermod Lynskey acts the role of a missionary to Native Americans during one Irish Fest program

Fans of the Irish language love exploring the Gaeltacht area in the Cultural Village, which calls to mind the Irish (Gaelic)-speaking regions of Ireland. In 2004, Irish speakers were impressed by the visit of Irish Minister Éamon Ó Cuív, who praised the presentations and performances, chatting in Gaelic with patrons and exhibitors alike.

Each year, the Gaeltacht display area invites several winners of the *Oireachtas* -- a nationwide Irish music and culture competition -- to perform. The Oireachtas is held in Ireland during the first week of November. After the winners are announced, one of the Irish Fest contacts in Ireland gives the area coordinators recommendations as to available invitees. Some of the winners have never been to Milwaukee Irish Fest and others are returning guests. The rest of the lineup is generally chosen through word-of-mouth and by being acquainted with dancers and musicians, along with *sean-nos* singers, those who don't use instrumental accompaniment. Some guests are invited to be included in special events, such as book and CD launches held at the Gaeltacht.

Major performers have included Meaití Jó Shéamuis, a *sean-nos* singer and whistle/pipe player who also hosts a radio program for RTÉ *Raidió na Gaeltachta* in Ireland; Ray Mac Mánais, principal of an Irish language school who performs

Aran Islands experts pass down their skills to fest goers

Dan Hintz participates in a storytelling competition during an early Irish Fest on the Children's Stage

verse and song in English and Irish and has won several *Oireachtas* competitions; fluent Irish-speaker Brian Hart, a native of St. Louis who is well-known for his *sean-nos* talent; and the Madison-based group, Navan, singing in several Celtic languages.

Fest patrons are invited to "drop by for a cuppa" tea and conversations in Irish. There are often opportunities to meet noted Irish authors and personalities who speak Gaelic, such as music scholars Fintan Vallely and Charlie Piggot. Led by representatives of *Conradh na Gaelge* and other Irish language groups, lessons presented in Gaelic are packed with participants. A traditional music *seisiún* might include Pat Cloonan, Seán Ó Gráinne, Aine Meenaghan, Dineen Grow, Brion O Broin and Frank Whelan. Keeping in mind the festival's mission of encouraging love of all things Irish by upcoming generations, the staging of *Na Trí Mhuicín* (*The Three Little Pigs*) was presented in 2005 for delighted youngsters in both Irish and English.

Gaeltacht coordinator Ina Kielley attended her first festival at age six. Working with Wendy Landvatter, a grown-up Kielley now makes certain that every performer in her lineup is well-informed about the what, where and how of the festival and ensures that all of the logistics are taken care of well ahead of time. The Gaeltacht schedule is normally set in November or December and most technical aspects such as tent layout and volunteer passes are taken care of before the middle of July. Then in August, the two can accommodate last-minute details and enjoy themselves during the festival. Planning for next year's Irish Fest begins within a month after each festival ends.

Street-performing, in which entertainers portrayed real and mythological Irish characters, was a major component of the first years of the festival. There were jugglers, poets, pubkeepers, musicians and high kings to keep the crowds entertained. The fight scene from the famed John Wayne-Maureen O'Hara movie, *The Quiet Man*, attracted plenty of attention in 1981.

Over the next few years, Druids Jeff Grygny and Bob Zimmerman kept festgoers laughing. Diana Sunn and Tom Placek acted as Brannon and Tomas, the Lenahan tinkers. Judy Lynn Zimmerman "became" Lady Galadriel. Femorians, those Irish giants of yore, were played by Mike Torti and Fred Swanson.

Jeanne Cissne, now the fest's accommodations coordinator, played the "White Witch of the West." This was a strolling character who put a blessing or a pox on guests. Cissne wandered through the grounds in her old wedding dress and a white witch's hat with a spangly green shamrock on the top, carrying a white curtain rod for her wand, reciting a ditty about being the "white witch of the Gael. If you listen at night, you can hear me wail." Then she later became the crimson-haired Queen Maeve, another roving personality appropriately attired in a flame-red costume and gaudy jewelry, while carrying a sword and shield.

During this era, Cissne also helped recruit young people for the children's theater by visiting schools and explaining Irish Fest acting opportunities. As part of the training, an apprentice program to encourage young performers attracted many youngsters like Becky Luterbach and Sandy Gennrich. Some, such as Stephen Hintz, had already studied or acted in other theater settings in Milwaukee. Many of the kids were then able to act under the direction of the festival's Kate Reilly in *Lawn Dyarrig and the Knight of Terrible Valley* in 1985, *The Fairy Ring*, presented in 1984 and *Meg's Gold* in 1988.

The first adult theater offering was put together by Walczyk in 1982, with John Millington Synge's *In the Shadow of the Glen*. The following year, three shows were presented and four were staged in 1984. Irish Fest reached out to attract talented Irish performers, as well. Chief among the early directors was the notable Dermod Lynskey, who along with Mary Kruser, Paul McGrath and John Gleeson, presented Synge's *Shadow* play again in 1985.

Lynskey returned to the festival for several years, appearing in numerous roles. He even portrayed a missionary priest in a program involving Native Americans who arrived on the lakefront in canoes. In 1984, Lynskey staged his James Joyce routine in the Milwaukee Art Museum, luring art patrons to the festival through a joint promotion between MAM and Irish Fest. The linkage there also included the showing of films and presentation of master drawings from the National Gallery of Ireland over the Irish Fest weekend.

Other well-known regional actors trodding the festival boards over the years have included Denis Regan, Dom Greer, Mary Kruser, Eamonn O'Neill, Frank Gleeson, Josephine Craven, Colleen Keenan, Chris Cedarburg, Tom Murphy, Michael

Pikuleff, Eileen Mullane, Michael Liston, Siobhan Dockery and dozens of other thespians.

Milwaukeean Margaret Rogers wrote several of the productions staged at Irish Fest, such as *Excursion*. The play, presented in 1986, told of the tragic sinking of the Lady Elgin steamship in Lake Michigan in 1860. Rogers also acted the role of Lady Gregory, the grande dame of Irish theater, in highly regarded performances during the mid-2000s. In 2005, local playwright/actors Edward Morgan and John Kishline brought that history to life again, with their rendition of *A Rising Wind: The Lady Elgin Story*.

The Irish Fest Theatre Company moved beyond the fest to stage shows throughout the year, even collaborating with such notable playwrights as the late essayist and broadcaster Steve Allen. The troupe presented his *The Wake* at the Milwaukee Performing Arts Center in 1991. This festival company became the nucleus for Milwaukee Irish Arts, which continues to sponsor a range of Irish cultural offerings throughout the city, as well as at Irish Fest.

"For a long time, putting on plays in a tent amid the din of a major festival seemed to be among the most exciting challenges I could imagine -- a reach-back to the medieval roots of drama, with the help of lavaliere microphones," recalled actor/playwright Dave O'Meara. "I had a chance to immerse myself in the work of great Irish writers such as Joyce, Beckett, Flann O'Brien, Synge and O'Casey, to associate with major contemporary Irish theatrical talents such as Chris O'Neill, Jon Kenny and Pat Short, and to support a legion of dispersed Hibernians for whom Irish drama was a profound connection to home. It was a blast."

Theater troupes from Ireland, Canada and throughout the States have also visited Milwaukee for the fest, including Chicago's Standby Productions and the Gaelic Park Players, Macnas of Galway, St. Paul's NaFianna Irish Theatre, the Tara Players of Winnipeg and Dublin's Celtic Dawn Theatre. Their professionalism and creativity have kept audiences returning year after year. In 1982, the festival hosted the elegantly gracious Mrs. Eileen O'Casey, widow of the late playwright Sean O'Casey, for a round of lectures and appearances that discussed her husband's works and the Irish

Dancers closely follow Jean Butler, a former *Riverdance* star, during a summer school class

Culture

Armagh Rhymers

theater scene. In keeping with the theme, cultural exhibits that year included displays on the Abbey Theatre, O'Casey himself and John Millington Synge.

The theater area also regularly hosts a film festival offering top features and documentaries from Ireland, taking its cue from Tom Cannon that first year when he organized an "Ireland in Cinema" presentation featuring three films: *Ireland: Heritage of the Past, Celtic Gold in Ireland* and *Land of Saints and Scholars.* Over the ensuing years, cinema lovers have thrilled to *Poteen, Inside Job, Boom Babies, Clash of the Ash, Schooner* and similar award-winning favorites.

Giving festgoers another chance to touch Irish tradition was the concept of the Hedge School, harkening back to Ireland's colonial days when outlawed teachers had to hide along the ditches in order to tutor their pupils. The "school" idea grew out of a talk in 1982 led by UWMers Gareth and Janet Dunleavy and Dublin-born pub owner Kit Nash, discussing Ireland and Irish culture on the same stage where the plays

were presented. Today, the organizers spend hours planning interesting, fun and informative programs.

The school now has its own tent in the Cultural Area, devoted to lectures and presentations on a broad range of topics which have included a chat about the rough and tumble world of politics by the late George Reedy, once press aide for President Lyndon Johnson; Irish American journalism by reporters and editors of *The Irish American Post*; and the role of the storyteller in Celtic and Ojibway traditions, by author Andy Connor. For the 25th anniversary year, speakers discussed Irish American immigration, the history of Irish Fest and the Gaelic Athletic Association, while writers such as Ray Mac Mánais, Larry Kirwin, J.P. Sean Callan, Connor Cunneen and Kevin O'Hara told about their books, much to the enjoyment of the crowd. In addition, University of Wisconsin-Milwaukee poet James Liddy read from his works.

Participants love the interaction between presenter and audience. "I took delight in venturing down the Old Claddagh of many memories. They really struck a chord," said Peadar O'Dowd, author of *Down By The Claddagh,* who presented a session on fishing villages in 2003.

One major component of the Hedge School is the reading of award-winning poetry, sponsored by the festival in a competition initially organized by the late Joseph Gahagan of the UWM English department. The Joseph Gahagan Memorial Prize is subsequently awarded in his name. Another prize honors Milwaukee writer/teacher/linguist Donn Goodwin, who collapsed and died on an Irish Fest stage in 1990 while reading one of his works.

In 1983, Jean Straub, a librarian at the Milwaukee Public Library, and Nancy Walczyk announced at a Shamrock Club meeting that there would be a gathering at Straub's home for those interested in planning a genealogy table at Irish Fest. The result was two eight-foot tables in the Cultural Tent,

Jeanne Cissne (far left) as Queen Maeve leads a contingent of Irish Fest wandering characters

Irish genealogy expert James Williams of Ennis was among the experts who have helped answer heritage questions

alongside the freckle and baking contests, lacemaking and storytelling. That small corner grew to its own 20-by-20 tent in 1985. In 1992, it was a 40-by-40 tent and on to a 60-by-60 tent in 1998. In 1990, Fr. Michael Maher launched an oral history project and the volunteers there started genealogy classes.

Faith O'Connell became co-coordinator of genealogy after being "adopted" by Jane and Bill Maher and their Irish Fest crew during that first year. Once together, they immediately told war stories about their searches for family roots and helped each other track down ancestors. When the Irish Genealogical Society of Wisconsin was organized in 1992 with Jane Maher as its first president, O'Connell jumped right into the middle of the action as a charter member.

Keeping track of a large number of volunteers -- from 10 to 12 are needed to set up the area -- and trying to keep everyone cool and well-watered remain important tasks for the genealogy tent coordinators. After a decade of assistance starting in 1993, the Library of Family History of the Church of the Latter Day Saints in Hales Corners, Wisconsin, which has an extensive genealogy data pool, departed Irish Fest. Yet the festival volunteers were able to carry on their work. Far from the days of pouring over paper documents, on-line research has become very popular with fest patrons who use a bank of computers in their searching.

Also on hand to help have been Dwight Radford and Kyle Betit, co-authors of *Ireland: A Genealogical Guide for North America* and editors of *The Irish at Home and Abroad*. In addition, genealogist James Williams of Ennis, Nora M. Hickey from Kinsale, Belfast's Fintan Mullan and Dublin's Dr. James G. Ryan and John Grenham, plus additional experts, have visited from overseas. In 2005, Kyle Betit, a professional genealogist from Salt Lake City, fielded tough questions about finding long-lost ancestors and festgoers attended classes in "How to Begin Your Own Family Tree."

Indicative of the tent's popularity, regulars return every year with their research and get help whenever they are stuck with some genealogical twist, turn or blind alley. Some visitors come in simply to inquire if their name is Irish and many more ask specific questions about an upcoming trip to Ireland. The genealogy crew heads to the grounds *en masse* on the Thursday of fest week to set up the exhibit boards, banners and books, plus lay out the floor plan, a process that they all admitted was hard work.

The Liturgy for Peace and Justice is an another expression of how Irish culture is promulgated. "The very fact that the celebration of Sunday Mass would be central to Irish Fest is a tribute to the fact that they have their priorities right," agreed Milwaukee Archbishop Timothy Dolan, adding, "That the fest would give centrality to that (Catholic) faith is a real tribute."

George Reedy, once press secretary for President Lyndon Johnson, lectures at the Hedge School

The visible expression of faith and community is magnified by the image of thousands of people of all ages winding their way through the city's Old Third Ward to attend the Liturgy on Sunday mornings. The streets are filled with cars an hour before the Mass begins. They come in rain and in sunshine. It is a reaffirmation of the values in the festival to see families with teenagers helping grandparents up the steep slope to the Marcus Amphitheater. People with canes and wheelchairs make their way along with young families pushing babies in strollers. The sound of 15,000 people standing up at once is like a thunder clash. It gets everyone's attention. The numbers have become so large that observers think the "miracle of the loaves and fishes" must take place to have enough hosts to give everyone the Eucharist.

Visitors appreciate the sense of peace and tranquility that the Sunday morning Mass offers. Its pomp and ceremony, music and the sermons -- regardless of the latter's length -- touch the hearts and souls of attendees. Occasionally a celebrant, overcome with the opportunity to preach to thousands, may produce an extended homily and resulting longer-than-usual Liturgy. This can result in several hundred volunteers furtively leaving early to get to their assigned posts before the festival opens.

The Liturgy is held in the sprawling Marcus Amphitheater on the festival's South End, with a signer for the hearing impaired always on hand. Longtime coordinators Bob and Paula Harrold ensure that everything is in place, that the singers are indeed ready and the vestments are laid out backstage. Testifying to their enthusiasm, the 100-member volunteer choir holds six, two-to-three-hour practices in the weeks before the fest.

Fr. Mike greets President Mary McAleese and her husband Martin

Thanks from on High

"We, the Holy Angels St. Vincent de Paul Conference and food pantry volunteers are indeed grateful for the invitation to again be the recipients of the foodstuff that we received from the people who attended the Irish Fest Mass…You and your staff are remembered in prayer at Holy Angels for the concern you have to assist in our ministry to those less fortunate than we are. Long live the spirit of the Irish."

-- Sister Jilene Giordana, Coordinator, SVDP Conference, Milwaukee

Milwaukee Archbishop Timothy Dolan

Mass celebrants have included Milwaukee Archbishop Rembert Weakland, who led services in 1981 and in 1982. The first Mass was held on the old Pabst Stage, with County Executive William F. O'Donnell helping bring up the offertory gifts. Among those following Weakland have been Bishop Richard Sklba (1983); Galway Bishop Eamonn Casey (1991); Auxiliary Bishop Edward O'Donnell of St. Louis (1992); Auxiliary Bishop John R. Sheets of Fort Wayne and South Bend, Indiana (1993); Fr. Peter Connolly, D.Ss.R., of Oconomowoc, Wisconsin (1994); Fr. Derrick Byrne, from the St. Patrick's Missionary Society in Kiltegan, Co. Wicklow (1995); Fr. Seamus Freeman, superior general of the Pallotine order (1996); Bishop Timothy Lyne of Chicago (1997); Fr. Thomas L. Knoebel, academic dean of the Sacred Heart School of Theology, Hales Corners, Wisconsin (1998); and Cahal Cardinal Daly, Armagh, Northern Ireland (2000). Jesuits with a Marquette University connection also celebrated the Liturgy, including Fathers Bob Purcell, George Winzenburg, Roc O'Connor and Michael Maher.

Bishop Norbert Dorsey of Orlando, Florida, the national chaplain of the Ancient Order of Hibernians, attended in 2001. Milwaukee Archbishop-elect Timothy Dolan was on hand in 2002, even before he was officially installed, and returned in 2003. Chicago's Auxiliary Bishop Francis J. Kane celebrated in 2004.

"The Mass was indeed the highlight of the celebration. I am pleased that is not a 'slapped-together' get-it-out-of-the-way type of celebration. It is very moving; as a matter of fact, the friend who was with me said that he has never enjoyed a Mass so celebrating community and so well-prayed," St. Louis Auxiliary Bishop O'Donnell wrote to organizer Paula Harrold upon his return home in 1992.

Many other clergy have also participated in the Mass. All the concelebrants throughout the years have been caught up in the sweeping ceremonies. "I was deeply moved by the liturgy and the faith of the many thousands who attended," said Fr. Kevin O'Neill Shanley who helped celebrate the liturgy with Abbot Eugene Hayes of St. Michael's Abbey in 1999. Although Shanley, a journalist/historian/teacher from Darien, Illinois, had attended many of the previous festivals, it was his first concelebration.

Special guests are often invited to bring the offertory gifts to the altar and participate in other ways. A festival highlight for Anne Melia of the Spirit of Galway tourism group was being honored on two occasions by reading the Prayers of the Faithful. For Mike Brady, among his proudest moments as a volunteer was the great opportunity to also read at the Irish Fest Mass several years ago and then to hear his sons also perform the readings in 2002 and 2003.

When in town, master of ceremonies and liturgical guru Fr. Michael Maher, S.J., of the Irish Fest family of Mahers, usually assists on the altar and helps keep the hierarchy on track. He also was the celebrant for the 25th year anniversary liturgy, at which Irish President Mary McAleese read from *Romans* 11:33-36, relating "the depth of the riches and wisdom and knowledge of God." The always-uplifting prayer, the *Kyrie*, was sung in Irish from a composition by the late great musician Seán O Riada. Sunday's total attendance of 48,374 was the highest in Irish Fest history.

From the second year of Irish Fest, the liturgy provided a perfect backdrop for encouraging attendees to donate food items to food banks. From this beginning, the St. Vincent de Paul Society and the Interfaith Conference were on hand to help gather up the goods. Festgoers bringing gifts prior to the liturgy are still given free admission for the festival's Sunday program. Subsequently, tons of nonperishable items are regularly collected each year. Several other ethnic festivals followed Irish Fest's lead and organized food drives of their own.

There are many more lighthearted "cultural" moments that are always fun at the festival. Some are probably not considered "really Irish," but no one really seems to care. Retired Judge Michael Barron has been tasting the best Irish recipes every year as a judge at the Baking Contest. He annually dons a pair of shamrock pants for the occasion. And the St. Rose Parish Community and St. Catherine's Congregation have been helpful hosting "Paddy Bingo," a popular place for elders to sit, chat and win prizes.

The Summer School, a weeklong immersion program of music, singing, history, dance, crafts, arts, genealogy and language, is one of the most important outreach venues of the festival's arts and culture program. The classes, held at the University of Wisconsin-Milwaukee, started in 1987 and were first led by Cecilia (Cease) Farran, followed by Jane Walrath.

Farran attributed the inspiration for the school to John Eagan, father of Sean Eagan, the talented whistle and flute player for St. James's Gate. Farran accompanied the younger Eagan to Listowel, Ireland, for the *fleadh*, Ireland's national music competition, immediately following the 1986 Irish Fest. At the competition, St. James's Gate won the first place All-Ireland trophy for ensemble playing.

Following the *fleadh*, Farran traveled with the band to Dublin and met the elder Eagan, a musician who had been so instrumental in the folk and trad music revival. In the 1950s and 1960s, Eagan hosted such luminaries as the Chieftain's Paddy Maloney and the Clancy Brothers in his home for regular Wednesday *seisiúns*. As Farran recalled, Eagan sat in his parlor well into the night, Guinness at hand, exercising his stiff fingers. He coaxed a fabulous sense of lilting Irishness in

Paddy and Liam Clancy participate on a panel at the Summer School in 1994

smooth Sligo stylizations out of his wooden flute in jigs, reels and slow airs. Interwoven with the tunes, he would rest and expostulate on music, musicians, pints and friendships.

In that chilly parlor on an August night, Farran knew immediately that Irish Fest would be the vehicle for transmitting the wonderful depth of Irish culture -- such as she was being enthralled with that evening. There in that Irish home, with the tunes washing over her, she saw it all clearly. She met with Ed Ward soon after her return to discuss the potential of bringing the best of the Irish world to Milwaukee, to continue the learning tradition. And so, the Summer School was born.

Since 1995, the school has had 4,565 participants, averaging about 450 per year, attracted by the Irish world's top Irish musicians, dancers, scholars and cultural leaders.

Current school coordinator Jane Walrath had high praise for her many helpers, such as Pat Sadowski who labors in the reception area serving tea and goodies to all. Sadowski also handles book, CD and T-shirt sales at the school and on the grounds at the Summer School booth in the Cultural Area.

Kristina Paris also assists with shirts and host committee. Kathy Schultz manages instructor housing and box lunches for students. Joanne Woodford prepares the school's informational brochure and website. Brian Witt and Nancy Walczyk makes sure that music and culture remain integral to the programming. Gretta Comiskey, Mary Hippler and the late Mary Lou Heck have been among the long-time volunteers. Denise Benoit joined the group in 2004, freshening the mix.

Parties, receptions, hallway conversation and impromptu jam sessions at area pubs -- such as the old Bodolino's across Downer Avenue from the university -- have been as much a part of the Summer School experience as its courses, said

Culture

79

Summer School Memory

"...I took tin whistle the first year of the Fest Summer School in 1987. I had taken a 10-week class through the UWM Folk Center the year before, inspired by Tom Rowe's tin whistle playing with Schooner Fare.

"The instructor was Fr. Sean Egan. I came into a room of flute players (including) John Ceszynski, who was about eighteen-years-old at the time and could play anything by ear. I played everything as a slow air because I had to read the music (nine years of piano at least gave me that) and Sean had hand-written the tunes so the sheets were rather difficult to read. After the first few measures of a jig or reel...I was lost and then Sean would ask everyone to play the tunes again at my tempo....

"He was so kind and I did love the class although I felt badly that I was holding back the real musicians!

"The second year of the school, I took vacation for the week and went to every class I could cram in..."

-- Kathy Schultz, volunteer at the Summer School

Potential carvers watch a craftsman

Walrath. Bodolino's owner always took pictures of each session and put them up on a wall for everyone to enjoy.

Instrumentalist, singer and composer John Whelan was considered one of most pleasant *seisiún* leaders who always made sure to play a couple of the slower tunes so the beginners could join in. There was always the undercurrent of etiquette of how many bodhrans could enter in at one time or if a non-traditional drum could be played. But it all worked out, with friendships made then still ongoing. Regularly, others from the broader Milwaukee Irish community have jumped in to make the students feel welcome. As an example, Tom Mills of the Milwaukee Gaelic League (*Conradh na Gaeilge*) hosted a pizza party and reception for teachers at the 1994 school. Such stories of hospitality are typical.

Though tied closely with the festival, the school is truly a separate enterprise that passes along the culture in every tangible way, asserted Bernie McCartan, the festival's attorney and ardent Summer School fan. "Where else can children perfect Irish dance steps with a *Riverdance* star while their parents learn about current events from a cabinet-level minister of the Irish government," echoed school coordinator Walrath of the 2003 appearance of dancer Jean Butler and that of Irish politician Éamon Ó Cuív in 2004.

Many noted performers and educators have participated in these programs in the week leading up to the festival. They have included Liam Ó Cuinneagáin and weavers from Gleann Cholm Cille in 1994. In the classes of 1995 and 1996, Máire O'Keeffe, of Tralee, Co. Kerry, taught the fiddle at the school and then performed at the festival. Well-known Chicago musician Noel Rice of Baal Tinne and his son Kevin have been regular instructors over the years. The list of participants goes on and on.

Kristina Paris became involved with the festival via the Summer School, when her friend, the late Jim Glynn, showed her a flyer advertising Irish flute lessons at school in 1988. She signed up for Noel Rice's class and thought since she was there anyway that she would take some other seminars such as Mick Moloney's "Women in Irish Music," a *sean-nos* class and one on Irish arts. She became hooked on the school's educational opportunities, wanting to continue her own music studies but found there were no teachers in Milwaukee at the time.

Subsequently, Paris drove to Chicago every Saturday to meet with instructor Rice. Soon she found a few more Milwaukee students willing to form a car pool. They took classes and ate at a new ethnic restaurant each week. After awhile, the driving became tiring. So Paris thought that if the one week of Summer School classes each year was so wonderful and that if she was willing to drive to Chicago, wouldn't it be worth trying to get the teachers to trek monthly to Milwaukee if she could line up students? So she called Cease Farran and received permission to contact all the students who took Summer School music lessons.

Paris then hosted the initial gathering at her house, with Noel and Kevin Rice as instructors. "I'll never forget the first Sunday. There were 22 students. My son's basement bedroom became the bodhran room; the living room had flute and tin whistle. Fiddle students were sent to Maria Terres' home. While we waited for our lesson, we milled around in my tiny pink kitchen, sipping tea from the many Celestial Seasonings boxes I had stacked on my shelf. Those were some of the happiest and gratifying times of my life. The monthly lessons lasted about three years," she said. Several of these students felt the need to play more than just once a month and gradually added additional practices. Rice then suggested the group compete in the *Fleadh Cheoil* music contest in Chicago. They accepted the challenge and found it very rewarding. During one summertime practice, a couple walked by and heard the music emanating from the open window. They knocked on Paris' door and asked if the musicians could play at their wedding. Thus, Ceol Cairde (Music of Friends) was born, performing at each Irish Fest since 1989 and many weddings since.

For Paris and others, the Irish Fest Summer School remains a real gem. It fills the goal of educating people in more detail about all that occurs on the grounds during the festival itself. Paris also fondly recalled the musical get-togethers at Bodolino's and now revels in the legendary musical parties at the Gasthaus in the UWM Union. "I remember a few very special ones...Eileen Ivers and Brian McCoy playing 'Star of Munster' at a very early *seisiún* site at Kalt's (restaurant). It was like heaven must be like," she laughed.

The festival has grown but still maintains a very unique closeness. "I think it is because people want to be there, asserted Paris. "They want to learn, enjoy, dance, listen, meet, laugh, play, eat, buy and visit. I think over the years, people definitely have learned more and more about the music. The Summer School is a big factor in that," Paris said.

"People are surprised when they find out I have never been to Ireland. I tell them everything I need is right here at the festival -- the music is what I love and there is so much right here in Milwaukee," she said.

Usually, a central idea ties together the Summer School package and events and displays on the grounds. The 150th anniversary of the Great Famine was commemorated in 1996 with lectures on the Irish Diaspora and its impact on American music and film. The curriculum for the 2004 school covered Ireland's island culture with its demonstrations of Aran knitting by Una McDonagh, a native of Inisheer. There was also an archaeology class led by Theresa McDonald, a resident of Achill Island, and one on Aran Island folklore by scholar Pádraigín Clancy.

The cultural treasures of Irish Fest obviously come in many special packages.

Students from Irish Fest School of Music in their first concert, 2003

Chapter 6

Behind the Craic

Grounds

Behind the Craic
Grounds

...Irish Fest Number 1... I had gone out the main gate for the opening. All I remember was that I had tears in my eyes as the people started coming in. It was a beautiful sunny summer day and the Irish flags were flying and fluttering in the breeze. An older man in his 60s came up to me. He didn't know who I was but I had a two-way radio with me. He hadn't been on the grounds even a minute and he came up and thanked me. Wow!

Ed Ward, founder of Milwaukee Irish Fest

The luck of the Irish has been with Milwaukee Irish Fest since its inception, particularly when considering the event's location. The fest is held along the wave-lapped, tree-rimmed Henry W. Maier Lakefront Festival Park south of the Milwaukee Art Museum/War Memorial complex. It is common for visitors to be amazed at the walkways, permanent stages, food outlets, restroom facilities, parking and other amenities that make up the locale on the shore of Lake Michigan. There's probably even an authentic fairy ring on the grounds somewhere. But don't ask information booth coordinators Don and Carol Clark, the location remains their secret.

Irish Fest leases the entire site, which is known generically as the Summerfest grounds, nicknamed as such after Milwaukee's annual 11-day music festival of that name. The visionary Mayor Henry W. Maier, who died in 1994, was the city's chief from 1960 to 1988. He established Summerfest in 1968 after visiting Oktoberfest in Munich, Germany, and envisioned a similar festival for Milwaukeeans. According to Maier, the fest would be one that would also assist the downtown commercial sector nearby. In 1970, the festival moved from its initial scattered sites to Milwaukee's lakefront, specifically to an abandoned 15-acre Nike missile compound.

Expanding beyond its role as the site for the annual music festival, Summerfest welcomed the first Festa Italiana in 1978. That successful event not only reunited the Italian

Festival site along the Daniel Hoan bridge

community, but attracted patrons from numerous other ethnic backgrounds. Festa's success encouraged the Germans and the Irish to subsequently launch their own events in 1981, followed with programs presented by other ethnic communities. By the mid-1980s, a long-term lease agreement was reached between Summerfest and the City of Milwaukee and renewed in the ensuing years.

The first Summerfest stages were merely wooden platforms raised on concrete blocks. The entire complex now covers 74 acres, of which the entertainment area encompasses 34 acres. A 24,000-seat amphitheater covers 11 acres and the balance comprises parking lots and roadways. In 1983, turnstiles were added at the admission gates, allowing for greater accuracy in counting attendance.

When Irish Fest opened in 1981, Tom Barrett was just going to the festival as a patron. The fest didn't realize that it had to have its own ticket takers and Summerfest would not provide them. Subsequently, volunteer coordinator Mary Otto grabbed Barrett as he entered the grounds and asked if he would volunteer to take tickets. "So began my career with Irish Fest. I was the first ticket taker," he recalled. Barrett went on to be the festival's treasurer and a board member, plus performing many other roles.

By 2005, there were five permanent stages on the grounds, along with food booths with kitchens and storage space and covered marketplaces for vendors. For its venue, Irish Fest erects 75 tents to accommodate additional programing, stages and sales outlets. Due to its size and range of cultural offerings, necessitating the rental of the entire lakefront

In the hours before the gates opened, coordinators gathered for an on-grounds meeting at an early Irish Fest

complex, Irish Fest continues to put down the largest footprint on the Summerfest grounds of any of the ethnic programs there. John Walrath made the beautiful "lighted rainbow" which adorns the center of the grounds and constructed the updated version of Castle McFest. Walrath, typical of the event's eager volunteers, took on these projects without being asked.

Milwaukee Irish Fest has evolved along with Summerfest, whose staff operates under the umbrella of Milwaukee World Festival, Inc. Meetings with all the ethnic festivals are held monthly in the off-season with Robert Gosse, Summerfest staff director of operations. There, they discuss facility changes, logistical problems and address other questions about the grounds. Everything has a separate rental rate, renegotiated each year with Summerfest. Irish Fest, as with the other festivals, also indicates what it wants for music and messaging piped out at the North, South and Main gates. These services are provided by Summerfest.

Summerfest's Gosse was effusive in his praise of Irish Fest as a "good tenant." In his view as operational manager, charged with protecting Summerfest's physical assets, the huge group of well-organized Irish Fest volunteers makes his job easier. "Irish Fest is well-thought-out and pulled off," he asserted.

During the festival season, in the month prior to Irish Fest, Gosse meets regularly one-on-one with Irish Fest director Jane Anderson to ward off any potential problems. From February, 1997 to February, 2004, Irish Fest's Chuck Ward had held Gosse's position.

United Festivals of Milwaukee, an organization of the city's ethnic fests, helps each of the lakefront events contract with various vendors for chairs and tables, waste removal and other fixed behind-the-scenes costs. United Festivals can subsequently negotiate for cost savings, as well as work on areas of mutual concern. However, each festival focuses on

Transportation volunteers stand ready to serve

creating its personalized grounds image through colorful banners, bunting and other decorations.

As early as February each year, Jane Anderson meets with the volunteer area coordinators to review their needs. On a blank map, all the tents are placed with their proper dimensions, locations of ticket booths are marked and other grounds details indicated. Summerfest then digitizes the map and provides copies to Irish Fest.

Anderson also has the coordinators design their interior exhibit or performance space, indicating changes from the previous year for computer hookups, lighting and placement of tables and chairs. This information is put into an Irish Fest "bible" that Anderson then shares with Summerfest, the volunteer grounds staff, vendors, the rental personnel and others who need to be aware of what goes where.

After all its needs are finalized, Anderson then orders tents from Karl's Event Rental in Oak Creek. Around this time, Anderson's son, Bill, a fest volunteer in charge of equipment rentals, passes out forms to the coordinators to determine their requirements for tables, chairs, draping and other special items. Aided by Tim Heck and Mike Walrath, Bill Anderson is also responsible for delivery and set up of chairs, racks, carpeting, tack boards, fans and other materials.

Then Anderson develops a schedule for everything happening at setup. She makes several visits to the grounds over the summer to meet with vendors and contractors. Two weeks out, she is on the grounds daily. Once the Irish Fest crew moves in on the Saturday prior to the fest, Anderson is at the site early, sometimes as early 4 a.m. for media interviews. During the festival, she typically leaves by 2 a.m. and is asleep the minute she gets in the car, regularly chauffeured home by her brother, Ed.

During the festival itself, Summerfest staff is hired on an hourly basis. Tom Kennedy, area supervisor for security, and Anderson meet with these supervisors and plan out the security locations. Many of the security personnel are off-duty police. In addition, the Milwaukee Police Department has a presence at the festival and is available to help if necessary. Up to 200 Summerfest personnel also clean the grounds, handling garbage pickup as part of a contractual arrangement with Irish Fest.

Milwaukee Irish Fest has been proud to be called the "Green Festival," working closely with recycling organizations. In 1990, the festival won a second-place honor from the National Keep America Beautiful Committee for a recycling project in which festgoers were admitted free if they brought clean food or beverage cans to the gates. The promotion was sponsored by the USS division of USX Corporation. Bill Heenan, Jr., president of The Steel Can Recycling Institute, a division of USS/USX, and John Risser, manager of recycling at USS, visited from Pittsburgh to help manage the program that was supported by Miller Compressing Company and the Keep Greater Milwaukee Beautiful Committee.

On the grounds during the festival, beginning in 1991 and for several subsequent years, the LepreCan Collection Clan -- a contingent of young volunteers -- visited the booths to pick up packaging and containers for recycling. In 1992, an exhibit from Dublin Bay and a Green Cross art exhibit from children around the world were included in an extensive environmental exhibition.

For its ongoing emphasis on the "Three Rs" -- reduce, reuse and recycle -- Milwaukee Irish Fest received numerous environmental awards. Its Greenwish Village, initiated by volunteer Margo Kuisis, continues to have recycling exhibits and games for youngsters emphasizing the environment.

Among the Irish Fest set-up crew is Dick Stroud, who retired at age 60 in 2004 from Sears Roebuck, Inc., after years in the home improvements division. When Stroud was named 1998 Volunteer of the Year, his crew congratulated him by coating him with cans of green Silly String at the end of the Saturday parade that year.

Stroud arranges for storage and transportation of festival materials and schedules the moving of the 2,000-pound Gulliver character from its warehouse home. He usually starts planning about eight weeks in advance of the upcoming festival, sending out welcome-back letters and schedules to his volunteers. Once on the grounds his crew works on set-up.

Bob Hamill is another integral volunteer, directing the pre-fest set-up volunteer workers. Hamill's crew is responsible for whipping the village into shape and ensuring that everything is ready to go in time for opening. Shortcuts developed by grounds workers have helped simplify put-up and teardown, such as streamlining the erection of the Murphy's Pub set in the cultural area.

Set-up and signage headquarters are based out of a small trailer parked on Parking Lot C under the Hoan Memorial Bridge. Irish Fest provides construction materials, decorations and most of the tools. Forklifts are essential for the heavy work and a fleet of golf carts saves wear and tear on the legs and feet. Several of the children of Irish Fest volunteers have become Summerfest employees in the summers. True to the Celtic cause, they take off the weekend to return to their volunteer duties.

The weekend prior to the fest, a semi-trailer packed with items for the cultural area is placed on the south side of the grounds. If there are enough volunteers available, the trailer's contents are unloaded. The following day, approximately 60 to

Kathy Wood, former Board Member,
delivering brochures

Preparing the grounds involves some heavy lifting

70 volunteers of all ages move equipment and supplies from the Irish Fest office to the grounds. After unloading, the Monday through Friday prior to the fest are used for setting up attractions The easiest job is skirting about 250 tables and the hardest is assembling the pub's hearth.

Volunteers also prepare the Marcus Amphitheater for the Sunday liturgy. This involves one crew on Saturday morning to place the risers and chairs for the choir and another to take it all down on Sunday after the service. This task has to be accomplished quickly to return the chairs to the pub in the Cultural Area because the fest opens as the Mass ends.

Drop-off of material for staging and exhibits is made at the North, South, and Main gates. The setup crew then takes the gear to the proper space for setup. On teardown, Bill Anderson inventories all rental items before Karl's Rental returns to load it.

The most difficult part of the job is getting enough volunteers for the Monday takedown. The fest has one week to set up and 12 hours to leave the Summerfest grounds so the next ethnic festival on the calendar can begin its setup for the following weekend. Irish Fest moves the equivalent of four semi-trailers to storage. Most of the displays, signage and other items saved for the next year are safeguarded in locked containers.

For the first three years of the festival, much of this was simply packed away in the home attic of long-suffering, but always accommodating, Mary Cannon, the festival's assistant director. Many jokes circulate that some Irish Fest treasures remain hidden away and forgotten there. Volunteer Brian Ward still mutters about climbing up and down the flights of stairs, carrying heavy poster boxes as a youngster alongside his father, Jack, who oversaw all the maintenance and set-up in the early years.

Coordinator of signs and decorations Mike Boyle and his crew make sure that the festival's appearance looks good. Boyle -- an admitted list-maker and organizer -- was recruited by friend Chuck Ward in 1983. He has been a coordinator for 11 years and served three years on the board of directors. Taking over erection of the banners from Cathy Ward and Ray Crowley, Boyle was aided by his cousin Dennis Fadeski, a solid Pole who had the good sense to marry Erin Regan, the cousin of Boyle's wife, Brigid.

After a couple of years scurrying up and down ladders to erect the festival's signature blue banners with their Celtic designs, Boyle arranged for a donation from Dawes Rigging & Crane Rental of a self-propelled manlift. He added Pat Farley to the team in 1991. In 1993, Boyle was selected as coordinator. His dad, Ed, also joined the crew in the same year. He was regularly assisted by his daughters Erin and Meghan, who started helping when they were quite young.

By 1997, there were six crew members which grew to 20 people working in 2004. A second manlift was also added then. Among Boyle's helpers have been Mick McDermott and Tim O'Brien; Bill Hanrahan, one of the original signatories of the festival's incorporation papers; Dan Malloy; and Tom Zimmer and John McGuire.

The decorations contingent has only four days to place more than 1,000 individual pieces such as flags, banners and signs; but only one day to take it all down and haul it back to the festival office in Wauwatosa where it is stored. If the banners are wet from rain, they must be dried out before being packed away.

The signs come in all shapes and sizes. Smaller ones are placed on ticket booths; there are also menus and directional signs; and 4 feet by 6 feet schedule boards for each of the 14 performance areas. Banners up to 4 by 20 feet that identify the larger areas are also erected. Probably ninety percent or more of the signs are re-used from year to year, but more requests come in continually. In any given year, dozens of changes are made and several hundred new signs must be made by signmaker Larry Gietl.

Gietl first became involved with Irish Fest in 1982. He was playing on an over-30 league softball team with Tom Kennedy who, along with his wife, Colleen, was running the Tipperary Tea Room at the festival. Gietl had just started his own company and was working out of his basement on North 56th Street. Kennedy ordered a banner from him that Gietl hand-painted like everything else he did at the time until he began utilizing labor-saving computers in 1989.

The Kennedys liked the signage, as did the rest of the Irish Fest brass. Subsequently in 1983, the festival started using Gietl's services for all of its signs. The Kennedys framed a dollar bill, signed it from the "Tipperary Tea Room" and presented to Gietl. The bill, the first buck he made in business, is still on the office wall in his expanded shops at 5300 W. Vliet St. Over the ensuing years, Gietl has made thousands of signs for the fest.

Gietl's creativity included a banner in 2000 identifying the "Paddy O' Club," a reserved site on the south end that the festival rents out for private parties. The illustration showed Paddy relaxing in a lounge chair, hoisting a beverage. In 2003, Gietl produced a sign for Keith Finnegan's Galway Bay broadcast that showed Paddy in front of a microphone, with headphones on his head. Gietl also made a sign for the Roundabout Stage, once located just inside the Main Gate. The logo there showed a confused Paddy as he attempted to negotiate a traffic roundabout, a highway interchange often challenging Yankee motorists in the Auld Sod.

Gietl also designed the paintings that turned a few tents on the south end into the "Ballyfest" cultural village, depicting storefronts with sponsor names which usually honor volunteers' families. The idea was to envision walking into an Irish village when entering the cultural area. Gietl painted the white vinyl tent sides to look like shops. Each siding is seven feet tall, which Gietl admitted threw the perspective "a little out of whack, but they still work." Most are 10 feet wide, with the pub storefront banner being the largest, at 20 feet wide.

The festival now has approximately 20 such storefronts in the cultural area. Designs are replicated from various Irish books and posters and take on the look of what the donor is trying to depict. In addition, near the Main Gate are the Doors of Donors, a display similar to the famed Doors of Dublin poster. The display honors major sponsors such as Aer Lingus, Miller, Pabst, Sprecher and Waltons and others.

The decoration work starts in earnest the Saturday before the festival. On the Monday before the fest, Boyle, his daughters and father repair anything that needs it and touch up some of the sign frames with a bit of paint.

On Tuesday, Boyle's entire gang goes to work, meeting at Ma Fischer's Restaurant on Farwell Avenue for breakfast and heading down to the grounds by 8 a.m. One crew takes a manlift out onto Harbor Drive to put up flags, while the rest work on the grounds.

Tuesday through Thursday, the manlift crews put up all the higher flags and banners, as well as assist in the assembly of the rainbow near the Main Gate and the castle in the Children's Area. A varying number of other volunteers scoot around in golf carts and personal vehicles putting up all the lower-to-the-ground decorations.

Mike Boyle and daughter Meghan

Pat Farley in the cherry-picker

The Boyle family continues to work throughout the weekend because there are always a couple of late projects. On Sunday, Boyle makes a comprehensive trip through the grounds, taking pictures of everything to aid in the next year's planning throughout the winter. Then comes Monday, with about 10 hours to strike, pack and haul back to the office what took almost five days to assemble. It's usually 7 to 8 p.m. before everyone is back at the Irish Fest Center to collapse over pizza and beer and perhaps a pre-season Packer game.

The festival grounds accommodate numerous activities beyond the music that require space, among these are the two primary sports areas and the Summerfest lagoon. Urban Park, a playing field just north of the Summerfest site adjacent to the lake, has hosted Gaelic football, hurling and soccer matches. With a handstamp, fans can come and go. The athletic events became an important part of the festival in 1982, with Jerry Cronin as the area's first coordinator.

Urban Park was also the assembly point for other athletic events over the years. In 1991, Columbia Memorial Hospital (now Columbia St. Mary's) and Irish Fest sponsored its first Top O' the Morning run, with 800 participants. In 1992, the event participation increased twenty percent. As of 2002, the Arthritis Foundation manages the run, attracting several thousand participants. Coordinating the races is Irish Fest volunteer Colleen Hamill, a runner herself.

Also in 1991, the Danskin U.S. Women's Triathlon drew a record 750 internationally known women athletes for the grueling swimming, biking and running events. In 1992, the event attracted almost 1,000 participants, who graded the Milwaukee leg of the triathlon circuit as one of the nation's top three such track-and-field competitions. In keeping with the Irish theme, festival tickets were given to each contestant and trophies named after legendary Irish heroines were awarded. Although rotund Molly McFest did not participate in the games, she and husband Paddy acted as jovial hosts.

Another sports area, where internationally sanctioned tugs-of-war are held, is sited at the far south end of the grounds near the cultural area. The tugs, launched in 1987, attract teams from around the Midwest, Canada and overseas. Coordinator Brenda Frary of Madison took over the scheduling after the death of original organizer Bob Sullivan in a 1993 traffic accident. Each year, a Sullivan Sportsman of the Year award is made to one of the tuggers. The matches are by invitation and much-sought-after by leading tugging clubs.

Offshore -- in the 22-foot-deep Summerfest lagoon fronting the festival grounds on the east -- the Milwaukee Irish Fest Currach Club hosts a regatta each year. Sponsors have included Meehan Seaway Services or the Meehan Family Foundation, founded by Daniel Meehan. The club's racing circuit includes Pittsburgh, Philadelphia, Albany, Columbus, Boston, Annapolis and New

Orleans, with teams from these cities often attending the Milwaukee Irish Fest championship rounds.

A blessing of these Irish fishing boats kicks off the series of races, sanctioned by the North American Currach Association. Participants eagerly compete for the Granuale Trophy, the major rowing award. The currach club also hosts an exhibition tent near the water. Displays showcase how the long, low boats are traditionally built and used for work and recreation in Ireland. A rowing competition between the Milwaukee fire and police departments is also a popular draw.

As hurling became more popular, teams from Ireland and around the Midwest attracted larger audiences. Clubs from Chicago, such as Harry Bolands, battled the Limericks in lakefront duels at Urban Park as early as 1982. Milwaukee teams began sharing the limelight in the late 1990s and brought in a new crop of young, athletic, coed Irish Fest volunteers.

"I first really got interested in Irish Fest when I joined the Milwaukee Hurling Club in 1998," said Matt Larsen, one of two hurling competition coordinators. "I had been down to watch our championship match in August of 1997. I remember it vividly. A couple of friends who were in the club were really trying to get me to play, so I went and watched the game at Irish Fest at the end of our 1997 season, and I was immediately hooked. I fell in love instantly. The culture, the people, the exhibits, the music, everything about it made me smile," he said. The club now has a display area showing videos of matches and exhibits of general information about the game, rules, positions and equipment.

According to Karen Fink, another hurling coordinator, as the festival has grown, so has the hurling club's visibility. Whoever wants to scrimmage at Irish Fest tosses their sticks in a pile, which is then divided up to make sure that each team has the same number of players. In 2002 and 2003, Larsen said the Milwaukeeans had "an absolute blast" playing against a Galway contingent that annually attends the festival. Joe MacDonncha, past-president of the Gaelic Athletic Association, the governing body for Irish sports in Ireland, also stopped by to participate in a match one year. Two ministers of state, Éamon Ó Cuív and Frank Fahey, have also played, as did Terry Flaherty, a female Galway mayor.

Others also enjoy the frenzy of playing. "I showed some youngsters how to hit a *sliotar* (hurley ball)...It made my stay. Milwaukee was my kind of town," wrote author Peadar O'Dowd in *Galway Now* magazine in 2004.

Gaelic football has also been showcased at the festival, with teams from Ireland often competing with GAA clubs elsewhere in North America. Among them have been the Donoghmore Gaelic Football Club, the Wolftones football club, Chicago Junior All-Stars and the Chicago All-Stars. Rugby has also attracted its share of fans, with teams such as the Milwaukee All-Stars battling the Wisconsin All-Stars. The Irish Fest Open Dart Tournament was held in a darters'

Brenda Frary coordinates tug-of-war competitions

tent for several years, sponsored by the fest and the Greater Milwaukee Darters. Competitors vied for upwards of $7,500 in cash prizes, with sponsors including Lowenbrau. Cricket demonstrations were even highlighted in 1996.

In 1994 and 1995, mental agility was as important as athletic prowess during the Potato Olympics. Held to great fanfare, the games were organized by volunteer and eventual board member Dan DeWeerdt, who began working at the festival in 1991. He devised silly events that included an obstacle course that required balancing a potato on a wooden spoon while "jumping" the Cliffs of Moher and kissing the Blarney Stone. A spelling bee that involved spelling various potato dishes was another popular event. Milwaukee Alderman Michael Murphy, whose parents were born in Ireland, hosted the Olympics.

Milwaukee Irish Fest is truly a family-friendly festival, designated as one of the city's favorite attractions by Metro PARENT magazine. The honor is due in part to the always-busy Children's Area. Teacher Kathy Kaye was the first area's coordinator, responsible for establishing its general tone and approach. Many of the activities that started under her leadership are still the most popular, such as the Pot of Gold fishing game, in which kids angle for prizes, and the potato people, spuds stuck with gumdrops. Up to 2,000 youngsters participate each year, supervised by about 100 volunteers.

Board member and former president Jane Walrath's first job in 1981 was aiding Kaye. After about three years, Walrath was was named coordinator, helping make sure there were fun experiences for kids with an Irish twist. While she was coordinator, the main volunteers were Bev and Jim Smith, Maggie Fischer, Kate Reilly, Ellen Croke and Nancy Bunkleman. The late Jerry Keeling started out acting as a king in one of the plays and then became stage manager for many years. This group was also involved in the planning programs throughout the year.

After Kaye and Walrath, the area was directed by Cathy Baker Ward and Mary Pat Russell. Over the years, the area has evolved from the much-maligned Moonwalk, an inflatable bouncing attraction that was the bane of early treasurer Jerry McCloskey's existence.

These days, youngsters -- accompanied by adults -- can create a mural of festival mascot Paddy McFest, build castles from Legos, fashion Celtic crosses from foam, weave fairy wreaths and hop along stepping stones in The Fairy Ring musical game. Storytellers such as Seamus Kennedy, John Bryne, Batt Burns and Celia Farran, plus strolling musicians and wandering jugglers, have perked up the grounds with their youngster-friendly presentations. Built by Bob Hamill in 1992, the Lilli-Putt miniature golf course made in the shape of Ireland continues to present a challenge for the under-age set. Young festival volunteers such as two of Hamill's children, Bobby and Sheila, lend a hand.

In 2005, a small stage was erected to honor the late John Bryne, a noted puppeteer who had performed at the fest for a number of years. Bryne, of Kalamazoo, Michigan, was killed in an auto accident in May of that year so it seemed a fitting memorial, according to Cathy Ward. "Entertainers would come past and put on half-hour shows when they weren't on their larger stages," she said. A tented coloring area for the kids was also added during the anniversary fest.

Children's theater remains an important way to entertain kids, as well as lead them into a knowledge of Irish heritage. In addition to highly acclaimed plays such as Sean and the Menagerie, The Frog Prince and Children of Lir, dance schools such as Scoil Roe Dennehy Irish Dancers and the Trinity Irish Dancers perform. Young participants from The Irish Fest Summer School, as well as those from Scoil Baal Tinne, have also showcased their musical talents. MacGregor the Pirate, Kathleen Mohr as the Pocket Lady, Ross Sutter, the Armagh Rhymers, Eddie O'Doyle and Timothy Flynn have also dropped by for shows at past festivals.

Potato Olympics coordinator Dan DeWeerdt (kneeling left) and Alderman Mike Murphy (standing right) join event winners

Lilli-Putt attracts young duffers

For the early 2000s, Tim Russell, who grew up as a volunteer in the Children's Area, became the Children's Stage manager. He remained on duty until college beckoned and he subsequently could not commit to the full weekend. He was typical of the many youngsters helping out in the kids' section. Under the tutelage of coordinators Cathy Baker Ward and Mary Pat Russell, up to 11 youngsters were helping there at any one time. Some were as young as five-years-old. Many went on to other jobs with the fest as they grew older and able to handle more responsibility. As an example in 2004, Caitlin Ward mentored with hospitality coordinator Jeanne Cissne and brother Sean assisted on the Aer Lingus stage. He did such a good job that he was asked if he wanted to join the crew during future festivals.

Kids can also enter the red hair and freckle contests, which are held in the Crossroads area a bit to the south of the main Children's Area. Many Milwaukee County judges of Irish heritage continue to volunteer as judges for these enjoyable events loved by proud parents and grandparents. Among the local officials are retired Chief Judge Patrick Sheedy and Chief

Judge Michael Sullivan, plus judges Doherty, Brennan, Konkel, Moroney and Dwyer. In 1994, one of the judges was disappointed that the Red Hair Contest was held at the Children's Stage rather than in the Crossroads Area. He was concerned that the lack of direct sunlight at the stage in the late afternoon made his job more difficult while considering the intensity of hair coloring. The following year, based on his recommendations, the contest returned to the Crossroads where the light was more pristine and Irish-like. It has remained there ever since.

The Dance Pavilion is another popular gathering area, where live music and knowledgeable, light-footed instructors such as Milwaukeeans John and Joanne Woodford welcome walk-ups for impromptu jigs and reels. The area started in 1987 as a tent with the Milwaukee International Folk Band, directed by Dave Kennedy, and Mary Duffy & Company.

Well-known bands from overseas, as well as Stateside, have played the pavilion's stages. Among the performers have been the Barefield Ceili Band, Kilfenora Ceili Band, Sliabh Notes,

Bohola, RiRa, Ceol Cairde, Moving Cloud, Public House Ceili Band, Broken Pledge Ceili Band, Brigit's Fire, The Last Gaspé, Curtis Crossroads, Boxty, the Sean O'Neill Duo, 180 and the Letter G, Swallow's Tail Ceili Band and many more. From 1981 to 1989, Kathy Mallon, was coordinator of the ceili area and taught dancing there before moving on to become a board member and member of the scholarship committee and coordinator for the Moore Street Market.

The Crossroads, regularly sponsored by Bunratty Mead, hosts beginning lessons for the *Haymakers' Jig, Rakes of Mallow, The Bridge of Athlone, Siege of Ennis, Waves of Tory* and other popular dances. For the broader Gaelic flair, concerts by the Chicago Caledonian Pipe Band, the Billy Mitchell Scottish Pipes and Drums and other pipe groups, as well as dance exhibits by the Caledonian Scottish and the Gillan School of Highland Dance were also held here.

Demonstrations by the Irish Setter Club of Wisconsin and similar dog groups are also well-received by Irish Fest guests packing the surrounding bleachers. When not showing off, the dogs loll in their own nearby Celtic Canine Area adjacent to the lakefront, well-shaded by trees and cooled by the Lake Michigan breezes. Most of the nine native breeds of Ireland are represented.

In 1990, Jane Anderson approached Milwaukee communications specialist John Moriarty with the idea of developing a travel display area and asked him if he would be interested in coordinating it. Moriarty accepted the assignment and set about contacting Milwaukee and Chicago-area travel agents and tour companies specializing in Ireland. Interest was immediate and the concept took off in 1992. The first travel entities that participated in what was called "Emerald Isle Tourism" were Ryan's Travel & Tours (Chicago), Aer Lingus, CIE Tours (Chicago), Brian Moore Tours (Chicago), Carlson Wagonlit/Top Travel (Oconomowoc) and Dan Dooley Rent-a-Car (New Jersey). In 1996, the displays -- under the title of "Travel Ireland" -- were moved to the far north end of the Miller Stage area.

The challenge for the travel areas each year is to ensure that returning exhibitors have booths, while at the same time accommodating new travel/tour companies that hear about Irish Fest and want to be a part of the buzz. There is an average turnover of about a quarter of the vendors each year After a seniority list is taken care of, requests for slots are considered for the next group of exhibitors.

For Moriarty, the travel area was best helped by splitting the exhibits into two locations, placing them on either side of the Main Gate. On the south side, Travel Ireland was set aside for all for-profit travel agencies, tour companies and car rentals. The Irish Destinations area on the north side of the gate was reserved for government agencies such as the Irish Tourist Board, Northern Ireland Tourist Board, counties Galway and Down, Giant's Causeway, Clare and others. Moriarty is aided by Kathy Rave, who is most closely involved shepherding the "Spirit of Galway" contingent.

The Irish Destinations concept was actually an outgrowth of that initial Spirit of Galway area, when Travel Ireland outgrew its area and the Galway representatives agreed to share their location. Major grounds construction in 2001 around the Main Gate installed permanent booths and on-site storage space for matériel, plus provided strategic exhibit structures for the festival's two anchors: Aer Lingus and Tourism Ireland. After visiting the festival in 1994, Brendan McMenamin of Aer Lingus returned to his East Coast marketing offices to encourage more support from his airline. Former Midwest sales manager Patrick Miskell also became an avid fan of the festival, as has Chicago station manager David B. McGrath. In 2004, there were 17 booths for Travel Ireland and 12 for Irish Destinations.

The on-grounds office remains the heart of the operations, managed by John Maher who brought a wealth of experience to the position. Initially, he ran the bank operation for the festival from 1981 to 1984, was festival president from 1985

Tom Kennedy Bruce Jensen

to 1987, an ambassador-at-large in 1988 and in 1989 was recruited by Anderson to manage the office following the "retirement" of Mary Ellen (Melon) Wesley Jocham.

For the last several years, he set up the office on the Friday before the festival. Maher is typically on hand the entire time the office is open until the festival begins. From the Friday before the festival until the end of the day on the Monday following the festival, Maher is at his desk on the grounds for an average of 120 hours.

Two-way radios have been used for communications on the grounds, starting with 12 in 1983. Demonstrating the growing complexity of the event, 67 were in use by 1990, 93 in 1995, 109 in 2000 and 131 in 2004. Maher has the responsibility of ordering, assigning, keeping track of and returning the radios after the festival is over. Only two radios have been lost in 25 years.

For Maher, the most fun about the office work has been the challenge of dealing with a variety of issues, often rapidly coming at the same time. The biggest headache involves finding a place to put large amounts of material delivered to the grounds prior to the opening. Maher and his crew must also deal with the many visitors who drop into the office. They praise, complain, or seek to use the rest room. Some visitors are lost, confused, want someone paged or wish to find or be introduced to someone.

As a result, there are many good stories about the first cramped quarters and the fly strips dangling from the ceiling. In the mid-1990s, a man with three large, brightly-colored parrots was escorted into the office by Irish Fest security. He was found on the grounds near the North Gate, offering to take pictures of patrons with his birds for a fee. He claimed to have permission from some Irish Fest official whose name he forgot, a situation confronting Maher nearly hourly. Maher radioed festival director Jane Anderson to ask if she had given the okay for a man and his parrots to be on the grounds.

"I was shouting into the radio because the phones were ringing, the parrots were squawking and the office was in its general hubbub. Now Jane was in a meeting with Summerfest officials at the time but responded that she had given no such permission," said Maher. The Summerfest staff overheard but misunderstood his question and, under their impression that Maher could get overly excited at times, later asked Anderson why he would be so upset that someone had brought his "parents" to the fest.

"The end of the story is that I asked our security people to escort the man off the grounds but not before I provided the parrots with water. It was a hot day and we always try to be helpful and hospitable in the office," Maher affirmed.

Obviously the office management has never been a one-person job. Among the dozens of volunteers who have helped over two-plus decades by grabbing the phones and generally directing traffic have been Gail Fitzpatrick, Bernie Beutner, Liz Heck Sanders, Kyran Hamill, Ed and Betty Mikush, Dan Banaszynski, Robert Kennedy, Rick and Ann Weber, Margaret Carley, John Hopkins, Mary Lou Hopkins, Brenda Frary, Gerald (Andy) Anderson, Vivian Hughes, Joan Mueller, Tim Donahue, Michael Donahue, Thomas Regan, Joyce Johnson, Carol Clark, Jean Peterson, Michael Johnson, and Joan Keenan. Youth Leaders also help out, including Bobby Hamill, Bridget Ward and Caitlin Ward.

Office volunteer, the late Mary Lou Heck loved such questions as, "Can I bring my dog?" "Will my 80-year-old girlfriend be able to learn the jig?" "When can I get in free?" "Can I bring a can of food per person?" "Do I have to wear green?" "Do I have to be Irish?"

No, one doesn't need to be Irish. But It is obvious that the work never stops in the land of Irish Fest.

Chapter 7

Peddling Spuds 'n Duds

Vendors

Peddling Spuds 'n Duds

Vendors

The hustle and bustle of an Irish Fest weekend is a concert rainbow, a family reunion, a good-time-gathering for folks of all Celtic cultural persuasions. Even friends without a hint of green in their bloodlines are guaranteed a good time.

Yet Irish Fest is also part Irish county fair and part food fest. To accommodate the stomachs and pocketbooks of more than 100,000 guests each year, tons 'o spuds, gallons of wine, hampers of scones, oceans of beer and herds of corned beef are served. Retail outlets peddle boxes of McCann's oatmeal, volumes of poetry and piles of handknit Aran sweaters. The offerings are as varied and delightful as equines at the Ballinasloe Horse Fair.

A volunteer since 1980, even before the first fest, Mary Cannon became food coordinator in 1982, replacing Jan Pergoli who helped out the first year. Although it was a challenge getting good vendors in the early days, the fest kept viable data and used a strong stable of existing food preparers who could recommend new outlets when necessary. Kathy Menacher was a big help for Cannon in those first few years. Aided by co-coordinators Tom and Marlene Wiseman, Cannon secured contracts with professionals who could readily prepare a flavorful variety of items.

The criteria was simple: find food that was interesting, tasty, had an Irish theme and was able to be prepared quickly to meet the demands of the increasing numbers of hungry patrons. The original 10 food booths and carts in 1981 have grown to more than 50 booths and carts in 2004. The Venice Club and Koepsell's Popcorn have been with the festival from Day One.

Since finding an abundance of Irish food vendors has always been a challenge, the festival encouraged non-Irish food vendors to be creative. Some ingenious approaches included Wong's Wok posting details on how the Irish and Chinese worked together to build the transcontinental railroad. Vendors renamed products. Helmut's Strudel called its deep-fried sugar twists the "Shamrock Twist" and Gourmet Cheesecake offered an "Irish Tower Fudge Cake." Then there was Famous Hometown Sausage Kitchen's "Irish Bomber Green Pepper Sausage." Other vendors retitled their booths with names like "Paddy Murphy's Onion Patch" (with deep-fried flowering onions) and "Mother Machree's Strudel" (strudels and sausage rolls). All of this creativity helped promote a sense of Irish fun, in addition to augmenting the more authentic Irish food served by ethnic vendors.

Food vendors were first listed in the event's program in 1983. Food was so popular that Irish Fest then developed a separate, put-in-your-pocket, one-page flier that listed menu items by vendor for each area. This helped boost food sales and was copied by most of the other ethnic festivals.

Early vendors at the Miller Stage included the Irish Baker of Capital Court, Saz's State House and Salico's. Over in the Children's Area were Gilles Frozen Custard, Robbie's SnackDragon and Super Pretzel. Hegarty's, Gimbel's, Tara Mansion of Oshkosh, Judge's on North and the Venice Club were at the old Pabst Stage. Ethnic Enterprises and Derrig's Irish Imports held sway at the Heileman's Stage. In the Marine

Bank Sports Area were Costa's Lemonade, the festival's own Tipperary Tea Room and Traverse Bay Fudge. Around the Folk Stage, hungry guests could sample delicacies from the Shorewood Village Bakery, Firelight Inn and Ovens of Brittany.

By 2004, vendors served Hawaiian shaved ice, gourmet cheesecake, yogurt, meat pies, corn-on-the-cob, fruit bowls and several varieties of the ubiquitous spud, among many other items. The favorite outlets continue to be popular Milwaukee-area Irish watering holes and restaurants such as Slim McGinn's, O'Donoghue's, McBob's Grill and Lynch's.

Leftovers are donated to Second Harvester, a nonprofit agency which provides food for the needy. Irish Fest was the first festival to start this practice, which has since been copied by other festivals. This has resulted in several tons of food being made available on an annual basis in a win-win situation for the festivals, the vendors and Second Harvester.

Winston's Irish Sausage of Chicago, located near the Miller Stage, has been a staple at the festival since 1982. The late Mike Winston, Sr. -- who learned the butchering trade in Co. Roscommon -- opened his first Chicago store in 1966. He was contacted by another vendor to supply product for the 1981 festival. Noting the volume sold at that first Irish Fest, the elder Winston decided to go on his own to Milwaukee the following year. His son, Mike, Jr., worked at the festival even before he could drive, sleeping in an old camper parked in one of the nearby lots.

From those early days, the younger Winston now peddles upwards of 1,200 meat pies, 1,000 pounds of corned beef and 3,000 pounds of french fries at Irish Fest, plus enough sausage to wrap around the entire festival grounds. While sticking to such tried-and-true items, Winston experiments with new products. In 2002, his food firm introduced Irish egg rolls, made with corned beef, cabbage and cheese. The item quickly became a hit.

"This festival is the easiest one we do. It's like the Taj Mahal, with a permanent building and concrete floors," said Winston, who is also used to playing events in which he prepares foods under tents located in open fields. He brings 15 of his regular workers from Chicago to work the stand, paying their expenses and accommodations.

When it comes to potatoes, no one knows the *Solanum tuberosum* any better than Patty Rios of the Irish Baker, who has served the edible tubers at Irish Fest since 1982. "At Irish Fest, you expect to have potatoes," she confirmed.

Drawn to the fest because she ran the Irish Baker of Capitol Court from 1981 to 1984, Rios now has two locations in permanent buildings on the grounds. One is housed in the Greek Village stand located near the Harley and Aer Lingus

stages and the other can be found in the Ethnic Gardens on the North End. Over the weekend, Rios prepares up to 8,000 potatoes at the first site and around 6,000 at the second.

Some are served plain and some with vegetables, while others earn raves for their stew toppings. To augment the existing kitchen, Rios brings in five convection ovens, sheet pans and other gear to quickly turn out the finished offerings. The operation is a far cry from the first fests in which her potatoes were baked in pizza ovens and rolled out by means of broomsticks.

Her children, Bill and Megan, began working at the stand when they were kids. They are now in their late 20s, as are several friends who have helped out for the past two decades. Husband Juan also pitches in. The crew braves the heat -- which often hits 120° in the rear of the stand on particularly hot August days -- and the long lines of ravenous patrons, some of whom return up to three times a day to purchase more potatoes.

It takes about 10 hours for the Irish Baker to set up, with the team coming to the grounds early on the Thursday of fest week. Although the costs for the potatoes secured from her supplier fluctuate and aren't confirmed until about two weeks before the festival, Rios has kept her prices the same since the mid-1990s. Many patrons pick up potatoes to go.

Many other ethnic choices are dished out for hungry festgoers at such food stands as Gojo Pelicaric's American European Foods. Pelicaric's family has been manning a permanent food booth on the Summerfest grounds near the Old Style Stage since the 1990s. Pelicaric, who hails from Croatia, and his wife, Lori, of German heritage, have five children who are regular workers there.

Lamb, roast pig, hamburgers, mozzarella sticks and chicken dinners are among the Pelicarics' offerings, with a firepit on the north side of the building used for grilling. The flames there alone make a show, as son Joe slowly turns the spits. It takes about three-and-a-half hours to prepare the 50 juicy lambs and 20 whole pigs, which are then served on heaping platters. The Pelicarics know their products, managing a meat market at 54th Street and North Avenue. "We love Irish Fest and the Irish. They love to stand around and talk. We get many repeat customers, too," said Mrs. Pelicaric.

New vendors always want to know how many visitors attend the festival. So coordinator Cannon attempts to prepare any newbies for a large influx, noting the many out-of-town visitors who eat two or three meals on the festival grounds instead of the usual one at most other events. Stuffed potatoes and Irish stew continue to be the best sellers. Vendors submit menus, which are reviewed and approved before contracts are returned. Throughout the festival, Cannon, Tom Wiseman and their staff monitor the booths to ensure that the quality of food and service remains high.

The busiest time for eating has traditionally been between 4 and 7:30 p.m. on Saturday. Generally, visitors appreciate the variety of vendors, especially those presenting an Irish "flavor." Food is a good moneymaker and it is obvious that festgoers are hearty eaters. The average per-person food sales are among the highest of any festival, including Summerfest, said Tom Wiseman, food coordinator.

There have always been a few unusual challenges. There was the time that Jack Derrig, owner of an Irish Imports food booth from Dearborn, Michigan, proudly declared he was going to "stay ahead of the hungry Hibernians this year" by bringing his own restaurant stove to the booth. Unfortunately, he neglected to measure the width of the door and the width of his stove. One hour before the festival opened, the ever-reliable Summerfest staff was using a cherry picker and front end loader to remove a window in the booth and set his stove through it.

For the dessert-minded, the tea room has been a must-visit since the early years with Tom and Colleen Kennedy and Margaret Ward and her brother Charles as its first proprietors. Running the food operations there was an incredible learning opportunity for the team. As inexperienced as everyone was in 1982, the first year for a tea room at the festival, they overcalculated the amount of product needed and had numerous whiskey cakes, tea breads, and shamrock cookies left over. Nothing was wasted, however. The excess was donated to food pantries and went on the road, being sold at Irish festivals in Joliet, Illinois, and at Birch Creek in Egg Harbor the following two weekends. This first tea room evolved into today's Tipperary Tea Room, started up by Colleen Kennedy and Julie Bolthuis, a brand-new volunteer.

In 1982, Colleen Kennedy's daughter Karen, five-years-old, broke her arm two days before the festival opened when her mother was off making all the pastry. She then spent most of that evening at the hospital, but still managed to finish baking by the time the gates swung wide on Friday. Karen's eleven-year-old cousin, Katie Ward, who is Jack and Margaret Ward's daughter, broke her arm on cleanup the Monday after the 1986 festival. The incident occurred when the clean up crew was having a race to see which cart could get to the dumpster with the most boxes.

The 1990 tea room also had its share of excitement when Bolthuis broke her finger on the Friday night at closing. It was also her first day of volunteering. She and Colleen were rolling a bakery cart loaded with shamrock cookies to the cooler. The ground was uneven and the cart went out of control on a slight hill. Bolthuis tried to catch it as it fell and she broke her digit. But, true to the Irish Fest spirit, she did not miss the next two days of the fest. Bolthuis continued to oversee the tea room for many years, followed by Diane Errath. Many of the volunteers have been with the area since its evolution into the Tipperary Tea Room in 1990.

Mary Rose Teahan & Shannon O'Malley
of Irish Imports Teahan's

Before the area was built into a permanent structure in the center of the grounds in the 1990s, the tea room crew used a portable screen house for its cake-cutting area. Assembly and takedown was truly a hassle as the structure became more tattered and well-worn from use. During the 2000 fest, a deluge of night rain caused the roof to collapse, a fact not discovered until the Tipperary types returned to start a new festival day. The house was used one more year, being held together by prayers and duct tape. Needless to say, current coordinators Liz and John Kendellen and the other volunteers who work the area appreciate their improved facility.

In 2003, the Milwaukee Health Department determined that the tea room volunteers needed to be wearing shirts with sleeves. As a result, volunteers wearing sleeveless shirts needed to change; however, they had no substitute clothing with them. So Kendellen contacted the volunteer tent for help and several appropriate shirts were delivered. One male volunteer was not about to wear a pink top, although it was the only size that would have fit him. Ed Heck, a North End stage manager, saved the day and loaned the man one of his own clean, extra shirts.

The biggest challenge for the tea room staff is managing the Sunday sale of morning buns, held around the time of the Liturgy for Peace and Justice at the Marcus Amphitheater on the South End of the grounds. The task of running supplies halfway across the grounds had become extremely difficult, so a cooler was added in 2004 to hold the product. Upwards of 150 dozen buns supplied by Nova Cena, formerly La Boulangerie, are usually gobbled up. A few years ago, the tea room ordered an overabundance of green napkins, a nicety still being used as late as 2004. In that year, one guest used extras as earplugs as she sat sipping her beverage while the music and hubbub of the crowd washed around her.

Kendellen uses a number of vendors to ensure that the tea room is well-stocked with sweets. Suzy's Cream Cheesecakes provides 110 cakes and 150 dozen bars. City Market bakes and delivers 250 dozen warm, fresh scones each day, as well as preparing mint brownies and two varieties of sugar-free

pastries. Great Harvest Bread Company turns out hundreds of loaves of soda bread and Crestwood Bakeries makes 620 dozen shamrock-shaped cookies.

Of course, beer always plays well at Irish Fest. In 1982, a delighted Fred J. Rubner, general manager of the Pabst Brewing Company, enthusiastically reported that the firm did a 14 percent increase over 1981, for a total of 304 half-barrels. His percentage of total business increased from 39 percent to 42 percent. With that success, Rubner indicated that he and his staff were looking forward to 1983. Bob Milkovich of Pabst also was a great pal of the festival. Among the Miller Brewing Company executives, Tom Fulrath was another early supporter. For Miller Brewing Co., Sig Wysocki and Dennis Boese have been long-time Irish Fest friends.

Mike Brady recalled shadowing a volunteer from Festa Italiana during one long-ago Saturday in the early 1980s to get a sense of coordinating the beer deliveries. Drawing on his political-campaign experience and special-event work, he in turn recruited 16 friends, not all of whom were close to being Irish. Brady told them he needed their help as bartenders for a weekend, as long as they agreed to have fun doing it. In those first few fests, the Miller, Pabst and Schlitz areas went through 300 to 600 half-barrels each, with the number rising as the crowds grew over the years.

Yet fest officials have always been cognizant of potential problems when it came to drinking and constantly urged that festgoers use good sense when imbibing. As treasurer and president in the 1980s, Jerry McCloskey initiated a popular designated-drivers program involving Miller Brewing Company and Mothers Against Drunk Driving (MADD).

The fest also learned that shifting the most popular performers to different stages throughout a weekend would keep the crowd moving, instead of parking at one tent all day. This measure has drastically reduced the need for security in potentially problem areas. However, the best beer sales are still tied directly to wherever the entertainment draws the largest crowds.

In addition, although Irish Fest peddles the most beer among the ethnic festivals, sales have leveled off since the late 1990s as health and safety-conscious festgoers began to drink more responsibly.

There are always good stories concerning beer. For Tom Kennedy, beverage area supervisor, the flood year of 1987 resulted in the best tales. Water was ankle-deep in some bars, he recalled. Nobody wanted to leave in the rain, nor could they get to the booths to purchase tickets. But the beer crews had everything they needed: customers, bartenders and plenty of beer. So Kennedy made the executive decision to turn everything into a cash bar. The bartenders simply threw the money into cardboard boxes or beer cups. Summerfest officials eventually officially closed the grounds because of concerns about water levels rising above the electrical boxes. "And the party ended," Kennedy lamented.

In 1982, during a series of rain showers, the Summerfest staff gave the Irish Fest volunteers plastic garbage bags to pass out to attendees as makeshift rain coats. A joke then made the rounds that anyone could tell which people were Irish by how they used the garbage bags. The punch line indicated that the non-Irish wore the bags and the real Irish used them to cover their beer cups.

In 2003, Miller beer scheduler Bill Ray and pal Jim Pringle panicked on Thursday's opening night because someone had locked the walk-in refrigeration unit and no one could find the key. Luckily, they had half-kegs in other tents that were "borrowed" until the situation was rectified. But they were scurrying around, hauling barrels by hand. "I'm old. It was hard work. The thought of running out (of beer) briefly crossed my mind. Not a pretty sight! As always, the problem was resolved without too much notice to our customers. After the commotion, I grabbed a beer -- that might have been one of the best I ever had," Ray remembered.

What would Irish Fest be without longtime friends Brendan McMenamin, former district manager of sales for Aer Lingus and now of Celtic Golf; Attracta Lyndon of Dan Dooley Rent-a-Car; Juan Landa of Landa-Cleary Travel; Tommy Ryan of Chicago's Ryan's Regent Travel & Tours; Mary Pat Flanagan, Midwest sales manager of CIE Tours International; the folks at Bryan Moore International Tours; Tom Dillon, regional business-development manager of EEI Travel; and all the other tour operators plying their wares in the festival's travel area.

Using the years of Irish touring experience totaled up among them, they field questions, banter with passersby and repeat the alluring mantra that Ireland has provided an exciting travel experience ever since St. Patrick vacationed there. From behind tables laden with fliers and brochures, they outline the best and latest means of getting around the Auld Sod.

Artist Mary McSweeney

John Raftery with Anne Raftery-Betzel and Jackie and Cory Betzel of A Touch of Ireland

Shay and Tracie Clarke and their children, Conor, Saoirse and James, of Blarney Irish Imports

vendors

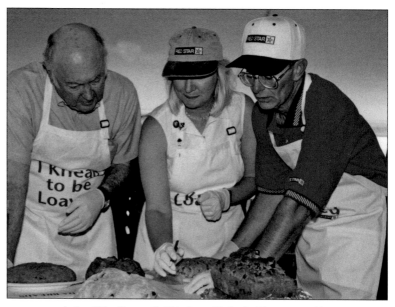

Jean Stemper and grandchildren Molly, Ian and Colin

Judge Mike Barron (left) helps with the baking competition

Participants appear to like the festival, said the hard-working area co-coordinator John Moriarty. "We've never had a vendor set up one year, then not come back because the festival did not live up to expectations," he asserted. New vendors are always amazed at the festival's size, although many have heard about it beforehand so they are ready for the crowds. In the early days, vendors occasionally ran out of literature, but they've fine-tuned their quantities over the years, to the point where they have designated daily amounts of print material on their shipping pallets. "These folks are pros for the most part

and they know unused brochures cost them money," Moriarty said.

But if the festival visitor can't make it to Ireland, the Grafton Street marketplace and the other sales outlets dotting the grounds provide plenty of opportunities to pick up a perfect wool shawl, pot 'o luscious marmalade, a box of McVitie's deliciously sweet digestives (cookies), a tin whistle or handmade silver bracelet. To make it easier for festgoers to enjoy their visits without having to haul around their purchases all day, package checking was introduced in 1984 as a crowd-pleasing convenience.

At the time the Irish festival idea was brewing, Margo Kuisis was employed part-time at Erin Ltd., an Irish import store In Mayfair Mall operated by Mary Ellen Simet. Kuisis had just given birth to her second daughter, Elisabeth, who years later would be honored as Youth Volunteer of the Year. Kuisis' good friend from college, Sarah Dann, also came to work at the shop.

Simet was approached by Ed Ward to suggest retail items that would be good to offer at the new festival. So her shop crew volunteered en masse at Festa Italiana to get a feel for what it was like to work at an ethnic event.

The women subsequently established a legacy of selling high-quality goods with Irish Fest's imprint, whether sweatshirts or raingear. Experienced retail vendor Bob Nolan helped most in the early years for bulk ordering. Later, more and more merchandise was selected from all over the world. For Kuisis and the others, it was fun to seek out new ideas. But from the beginning, the goal was to have the festivalgoers promote the festival through the purchase of product that had "Milwaukee Irish Fest" and the logo featured prominently. This merchandise helped brand the festival.

Each year, the planners came up with exciting new goods that were shown off at festival meetings to the collective oohs and aahs of those in attendance. Naturally, some goods sold better than others, resulting in chuckles, as well as occasional overstock. In 1987, Belleek plates with Paddy McFest's smiling face were introduced with a great deal of fanfare and anticipation. Yet much to the dismay of the marketplace folks, the pieces languished on the shelves for several seasons before finally they were all sold, and now they are collector's items on eBay.

Rick and Kathie Henderson of
Celtic Images

The creation of two retail spots would later expand to four huge Irish stores. Creating the stores before the fest opened, manning them and then taking everything down and inventorying the goods was physically demanding and necessitated good organizing and marketing skills. Hours of preparation were needed before stepping foot on the grounds. That, added to training volunteers who had never worked retail, much less a cash register, made the task challenging, exhausting and exhilarating. It was definitely a job for the young, the strong, the dedicated and the adventuresome. Katie Ward Mayes, who is currently co-coordinator of the area with her mother, Margaret, grew up working Irish Fest retail. Now, the extended family is involved in running the many booths.

Nothing yet fazes the marketplace crew, even wet or cold weather. During the former, rain ponchos sell well. With the latter, there is a run on sweatshirts. No one slows down, even during a flood year like 1987. That year, Barb Tyler and Colleen Kennedy organized a team of coordinators that included Julie Bolthuis, Kathy Rave, Maureen Murphy Modlinski, John Moriarty and Margaret and Jack Ward to rush to a laundromat on Bluemound Road where they spent the wee hours of Sunday morning monopolizing almost all the dryers to salvage damp goods. At 4:30 a.m., Kennedy treated the crew to food at a near-by George Webb's restaurant, paying the bill in rolls of quarters left from the laundromat!

Small promotional items always do well, especially for youngsters seeking great deals for their loose change. Weepuls -- small green puffballs with googly eyes, antennae, tiny feet with adhesive for sticking everywhere and a tag that read "Irish Fest" -- were among the most popular low-end items sold in the early 1980s. Kathy Otto recalled storing marketplace merchandise in the attic of her mother's house and it seemed as if they would never be rid of the critters.

Eventually, the family was sure that only a handful of the little green guys remained. "But when we opened the box the next year, it was full of weepuls, almost as if they had multiplied on their own," Otto remembered. Longtime volunteers still occasionally find a weepul smiling back at them from the back of a long-unopened drawer. A giant weepul has a place of honor, proudly perched on a shelf in the Archives.

The dramatic change in quality of merchandise demonstrated the festival's maturing. However, 2005 shoppers still had fun looking over a display showcasing 25 years of fest fashions ranging from suspenders to hats and other souvenirs. In honor of the 25th season, a music CD, *Silver*, featured 35 tracks of the festival's favorite performers. Waterford Crystal also produced a limited edition commemorative ornament and a paperweight which could be signed by a master craftsman from the company's Irish factory.

Larry Gietl and Marie Cramer

vendors

Linda Barry and her daughter, Cecilia, of Paddy's on the Square

Shopping for bodhrans at Waltons

Yet fest patrons seeking high-end items have long found extra special offerings well beyond green T-shirts. Among them are the copper and enamel designs from the *Book of Kells* originally produced by the late Gerry Forde of Louisville, Kentucky. Some of his pieces sold for $700 to $900. His son now carries on this unique craft tradition. Quality linens, sweaters, photography and artwork remain popular.

Vendors such as Milwaukee's Marie Stemper return year after year to what they agree is the largest Irish marketplace in the States, with a long waiting list for any open slots which are few and really far between. The marketplace denizens appreciate the fact that the fest attempts to limit the number of item duplications.

Many booth operators come from the Chicago area, not only lured by the proximity of the Milwaukee event, but the fact that they agree it is the biggest and best Irish event anywhere. Chicago's John Raftery of Touch of Ireland was told about Irish Fest by longtime-vendor/friend Peter Farley. "I was dumbfounded when I came years ago," Raftery laughed. "They do one helluva job here, they look after you well." For a time, his stand was known as the place to go for Irish dance shoes, selling dozens of pairs over a festival weekend.

Marie Cramer has been a vendor at Irish Fest since 1983, selling high-end sweaters, jackets and other knitwear to customers not afraid of spending money. "They come here to check prices and see that we can't be beaten," she smiled from behind her goods-crowded booth. Mary Rose Teahan, of Irish Imports Teahan's, is another pleased longtime vendor who has a satisfied and extensive roster of regulars. "They love tweeds," she enthused.

Shay Clarke and his family sell Celtic jewelry at 28 festivals around the country each season, in addition to operating several gift shops called Blarney: Everything Irish in the Chicago suburbs. He first set up his stall at Irish Fest in 1987, a month after emigrating from Ireland. "I had never been to Irish Fest before and my jaw dropped. There is still nothing like it, it's the biggest and best-organized in the world," he said. Serving a generation of customers, Clarke has sold claddagh rings to teenagers and, in turn as those patrons grew older, sold them their wedding bands.

Marylanders Rick and Kathie Henderson of Celtic Images Photography finally retired in 2004 after 15 years at Irish Fest. "We love the people here, getting to know them so well over the years," Kathie indicated. Buoyed by regulars who purchased artwork from them over the years, they lamented the fact that they would no longer have a sale presence at the event.

Irish Fest volunteers get into the act, as well. Seamstress Diane Stroud has become the official T-shirt shortener. Since the early 2000s, she has brought her sewing machine to the grounds to perform last-minute nips and tucks because the retail T-shirts are generally men's sizes and are too long for many of the women. Along with her daughter Shannon, and the other volunteers helping with the Celtic Christmas Boutique, Stroud also makes crafts during the year to sell at the annual pre-holiday bazaar at the Irish Fest Center.

There is always an interesting, and often poignant, story behind an Irish Fest facade. Cecilia (Cease) Farran's musician son Brian was recovering physically and emotionally from a car accident that took the life of his best friend in May, 1992. He threw himself into his cosmic tie-dye creations that were vivid and unusual, capturing the attention of Ed Ward who hooked him up with retail coordinator Margo Kuisis. She had him create 144 shirts that were sold out in conjunction with the US Steel Great American Hootenanny on the grounds that year. As recently as 2002, those shirts could still be spotted around the grounds.

The Moore Street Market in the Cultural Area brings in cottage industry artisans with special talents that are of cultural significance. Coordinator Kathy Mallon only uses the vendors for two consecutive years in order to encourage exposure to a variety of crafts. While at the festival, the artisans explain their skills, as well as selling their wares. The many artists over the years have included Lisa Davies, a jeweler from Colorado; basketmaker Vincent McCarron from the Aran Islands; bodhran-maker Malachy Kearns; knitter Fran Ryan of Dingle; Arkansan potter Robin MacGrogan; and pipemaker Ethel Kelly of Knockcroghery.

Artist Kevin Dillon of Coldwater, Ontario, sold his medieval and Celtic illuminated cards at the fest in the mid-1990s and attributed his appearances there for his ongoing retail success. "(It) was in large part because of the venue you provided me to market my work...without your show and the wonderful way it brings the public-at-large in touch with artists' works, I would not still be working at my craft today."

Few festgoers leave the grounds without a CD or tape from one or another of their favorite entertainers. The official Irish Fest album booth always does a resounding business, often selling out the hottest groups, as well as the old favorites. Gaelic Storm remains the all-time best seller, followed by Tommy Makem and Liam Clancy. At least one person per shift at the booth knows more than average about the Irish music scene. That is an important skill because the volunteers there often get questions such as, "I don't know the name of the song or the name of the artist, but it's about a river in Ireland. Do you have it?"

Originally managed by the late Jack Early and his wife, Mary, the stand was eventually taken over by the O'Connell clan. Early built the first album booth to fit the original confines of a space within one of the marketplace buildings. Tom O'Connell, now a board member and area supervisor for all Irish Fest sales outlets, remembered that the unit had so many heavy, gerryrigged parts that it was a yearly exercise to set up and disassemble. Eventually, O'Connell and his brother, Rich, designed a sales counter that was easier to move. "Still, I sort of miss the old album booth and its nooks and crannies," he said.

Judging from all this vendor activity, it wouldn't be surprising if Irish Fest didn't have its own horse fair someday.

Fergus Laly, *The Quiet Man* Collection

Peggy and David Michaeleon

Des Kenny talking books

Chapter 8

Irish President Mary McAleese and husband Dr. Martin McAleese
visit Irish Fest

Playing the Irish Links

Homeland Connections

Playing the Irish Links

Homeland Connections

"Irish Fest is almost too much for the human mind to take in."

Harry Bradshaw, traditional-music chronicler
Radio Telefís Éireann (RTE)

From its inception, Milwaukee Irish Fest has had close ties to Ireland, most notably through the promotion of music. After all, Dublin crooner Danny Doyle once said that playing Irish Fest was "like going to heaven for the weekend."

"Anybody who is anybody has appeared at Irish Fest over the years," stressed Harry Bradshaw, a traditional-music historian and a producer for *Radio Telefís Éireann* (RTE), the Irish public-service broadcasting organization. Bradshaw has visited the festival six to seven times to lecture at the Summer and Hedge schools. During his first visit in 1994, he taught a class on Michael Coleman, the noted 19th century Irish American fiddler.

Bradshaw first heard about Irish Fest while lecturing on Coleman at the Willy Clancy Summer School in Co. Clare in 1993. Popping up in the audience was John Gleeson, a Dubliner turned Milwaukeean who had previously worked in films with Bradshaw. Gleeson asked the historian if he would be interested in attending the next year's fest. Bradshaw indicated that he would be delighted. From that initial contact, an admirable union was formed.

In 1999, with funding from the Irish Fest Foundation, he helped launch the Traditional Music Center (Ceol) at Smithfield Village in Dublin and -- working with Irish Fest entertainment coordinators -- brought over singer/banjo player Mick Moloney and fiddler Liz Carroll, guitarist Zan McLeod, piper Jerry O'Sullivan and accordion impresario John Williams to perform at its opening. The musicians, all of whom had regularly entertained at Irish Fest, were also recorded for Irish radio.

Bradshaw and Irish Fest also worked with Aer Lingus to provide an inflight program using material recorded at the festival. The program was heard by thousands of the airline's passengers in the mid-1990s. Because the tape included contact details, the fest subsequently received numerous requests for additional information.

There are other levels of Auld Sod linkage, as well, including vendors in the marketplace, visits by political and cultural leaders and media coverage. In 1984, Michael Roberts, manager of the North American office of the Northern Ireland Tourist Bureau, sent 30 posters and promotional

Meeting with Irish Prime Minister Albert Reynolds were John Maher, Ann Comer and Jane Anderson

Meeting Irish President Mary Robinson (center) in Dublin were (left) Tom Barrett, Jane Anderson, Colleen Kennedy and Chuck Ward

British Consul Andrew Seaton and Vice Consul Caroline Cracraft

Connections

105

Ald. Michael Murphy presents a proclamation to Minister Éamon Ó Cuív in 1999

Kimberly Curry and Ilana Harlow from the Library of Congress and Allison Doolittle from the Dublin, Ohio, Irish Fest with Ed Ward

In 2001, Galway Mayor Donal Lyons was interviewed at Irish Fest by Keith Finnegan of Galway Bay FM

brochures entitled *From Here to the White House* for distribution. He also attended the fest, saying, "I need to see for myself what the festival is like."

The festival has enjoyed support from the Irish government over its full 25 years. This encouragement and backing has been instrumental in helping build the event's reputation as a festival that goes well beyond paddy-wackery and shamroguery. Irish Fest has never been a Green Beer Bash but an event in which Ireland's heritage remains paramount. The Irish government, whether on the national, county or municipal levels, opens doors, suggests exhibits, provides grants and generally helps cheerlead for the fest at home and abroad. There was great excitement in the Irish Fest community when it was learned that Mary McAleese, president of Ireland, was to attend the event in 2005. Months of eager planning went into preparing for her visit which included a major address at the festival and participation in the Sunday Liturgy for Peace. She also appeared at City Hall alongside Mayor Tom Barrett. A reception at the University of Wisconsin-Milwaukee showcased McAleese's announcement of a funding increase for the Irish language program at the school's Center for Celtic Studies.

The importance of the festival was noted by McAleese when she reiterated that "Irish Fest is known at home in Ireland as one of the biggest and most popular celebrations of Irish culture anywhere in the world." She cited the thousands of Irish musicians, language enthusiasts, arts and craftsworkers "who have passed through these gates in the last 25 years," pointing out how through the experience of Irish Fest that the global Irish family has grown closer and stronger, as had the shared culture between Ireland and the United States.

With the president during her Milwaukee experience were Noel Fahey, Irish ambassador to the United States, and other Irish officials. However, while the president's visit was noteworthy and headline grabbing, Irish Fest has long maintained a strong relationship with the Irish consulate staff in Chicago and other government entities "back home." For instance, Consul General Charles Sheehan and Vice Consul Úna Ni Dhubhghaill provided much assistance behind the scenes for the president's visit in 2005.

Consul General Conor Barrington spoke at the first Irish Fest, helping with the opening program in 1981 along with local dignitaries. In 1984, Consul Liam Canniffe and the festival discussed the potential of a trade show to promote Irish companies and to provide information on industrial and economic development in Ireland. Although the discussion extended to include Eileen McGrath and other officials at the Irish Export Board, a full-blown exhibition never panned out.

However, the Irish diplomatic staff has always appreciated the fact that Irish Fest so strongly pitches everything Irish. "We have reason to be grateful for your service over many years in honor of your heritage," offered Consul General Charles Sheehan, in praising festival founder Ed Ward for being named by *Irish America Magazine* as one of the top 100 Irish Americans in 2004. Ward received the kudos for his work in establishing the fest and promoting Ireland's musical heritage.

Award winning photographer Brenda Fitzsimons of the Professional Press Photographers of Ireland and Liam Clancy look over the noted musician's latest book

Consul General Gary Ansbro was always a good friend of Irish Fest and often brought other dignitaries with him to Milwaukee. "Both my official Irish colleague and I were very impressed by the fest's tremendous range of activities and musical entertainment and by the imagination and organization which went into it," he said following a 1990 visit.

Rory Montgomery, vice consul in 1992, performed his official welcoming duties at the Great Ceili early in the fest and then appreciated having the rest of the afternoon to concentrate on the music and "on some of the cornucopia of other attractions." He was especially taken by the Year of the Harp celebration, featuring the Belfast Harp Orchestra, calling the performance he saw "splendid musically and quite fascinating from a historical point of view."

In the mid-1990s, Consul General Frank Sheridan always had a grand time in Milwaukee and ensured that bureaucratic doors swung open back home, as necessary. "The fest was a veritable feast of music and culture, the setting was magnificent, the organization was superbly professional, the company wonderful and the *craic* (the fun) was great," he said after the 1994 event.

During his many visits to the festival, Sheridan reveled in performances by Frank Patterson, Sharon Shannon, Schooner Fare, the Clancy Brothers and Robbie O'Connell, De Dannan, Annette Griffin, the Black Brothers, Hal Roach, the Makem Brothers and Brian Sullivan, the House Band and the Great American Hootenanny, among the numerous local and regional groups. Consul General Eamon Hickey also appreciated the warm hospitality shown him during his visit to the 2000 event. "This was a wonderful weekend, worthy in every way of Irish Fest's 20th anniversary," he said, adding that his visit was enhanced by meeting Cahal Cardinal Daly

of Armagh who celebrated the Liturgy for Peace and Justice that year.

When she was based in Chicago, Irish Vice Consul Fiona Flood became one of Irish Fest's greatest fans and supporters, assisting with many behind-the-scenes activities in her role promoting Irish arts. One of her more visible tasks was escorting Irish Minister Éamon Ó Cuív when he first visited the city in 1999 as head of the Department of Arts, Heritage, Gaeltacht and the Islands.

While in Wisconsin that year, the Irish contingent also toured the pioneer homestead of Jeremiah Curtin, one of the state's Irish pioneers who was a scholar, diplomat and author. The ever-vivacious Flood thanked the fest for its "energy and professionalism (that) helped make the visit an unqualified success. I know that the Minister thoroughly enjoyed his visit and was very encouraged to see Irish culture flourishing in Milwaukee."

With the title of Minister for Community, Rural and Gaeltacht Affairs, Ó Cuív again visited Milwaukee Irish Fest in 2003, 2004 and 2005. He lectured at the Summer School, strolled the grounds, visited Irish marketplace vendors, played hurling, spoke Irish and shook dozens of friendly hands. He cited the awareness of the festival within the Irish media, particularly that of the Irish language press because of the festival's Gaeltacht in the Cultural Area and the emphasis on the island's arts. "There are a huge number of people aware of what the festival does," he said.

Prior to his first visit, Ó Cuív admitted that he was puzzled about why Milwaukee was hosting the world's largest Irish cultural event. "I admit I was surprised when I came here. Who would have thought Milwaukee!" he asked. But after spending long weekends roaming the grounds and talking to festgoers, he was quick to praise the committed group of volunteers that make the festival work so well.

"That organizational side of the event is so crucial," he pointed out. "It's easy enough to volunteer for two to three years, but 20 years or more is amazing," he said. Ó Cuív indicated that he would like to see the connections between Ireland and the festival grow even stronger. "I am all the time very conscious of strengthening Irish culture both at home and abroad," he affirmed.

Ó Cuív thanked the festival officials after his 2003 visit while accompanied by Consul General Charles Sheehan. "I was very impressed with the sheer scale of the fest, and the friendliness and enthusiasm of all the staff involved, especially the volunteers. The fest is an impressive showcase for Ireland, as well as a fun event, and as a member of the Irish government, I would like to thank all of you for your contribution to the success of the event," Ó Cuív indicated.

Connections

(l-r) Keith Finnegan, Galway Mayor John Mulholland, Governor Tommy Thompson, Clem Walsh, and Gerry Rabbitt, 1996

Tom Dillon, Irish Consul General Gary Ansbro and Ken Horan

Nancy Larkin-Rau of Bunratty Meade, Minister Éamon Ó Cuív and current Irish Consul General Charles Sheehan

Whenever Irish dignitaries visit the festival, they head to the Irish Destinations area to meet with constituents, talk business and get caught up on old friendships. Minister Éamon Ó Cuív considered it essential to visit the displays, talk about the exhibits and encourage the vendors. "We have to be conscious of what attracts tourists to Ireland," he said, citing the green landscape, the ease with which visitors can meet the locals and the many other attractions that draw tens of thousands of guests to his homeland every year. "We want them to come and experience Ireland," he asserted.

Ó Cuív emphasized that while every department in the Irish government had its own special interests, anything that promoted Ireland was beneficial. Since all ministers actively help with marketing their country's travel pluses, Ó Cuív felt it important that Irish Fest continue to highlight so many travel organizations and companies and emphasized that the festival's efforts merited support from the homeland.

Development of the Travel Ireland exhibit area came about as a combination of requests from travel agents and tour operators, and also requests by festgoers for more information about traveling to Ireland. The tourism component of Irish Fest kicked off in the mid-1990s after Galway resident Gerry Rabbitt was escorted to the fest by a friend, John McGourthy, in 1994. He was so impressed that on his return to Galway, Rabbitt decided to organize a group to come back the following August.

He called on local tourism officials and city and county officers. From their enthusiasm, the Spirit of Galway group was formed. Irish Fest is the only consumer show that the organization attends in the United States, although it participates in a trade event organized annually by Tourism Ireland.

One of those Rabbitt talked with was broadcaster Keith Finnegan of Galway Bay FM, saying, "Finnegan, we have to go to Milwaukee." From there, the relationship began.

In August, 1995, a group of approximately 55 people traveled to Milwaukee, not knowing what to expect when they landed in Chicago. Finnegan pointed out, "We were all tired after the journey and for some it was their first time in the United States. I remember it so clearly, we were booked into the Milwaukee Athletic Club and, when we arrived, we felt like we had just arrived home with the greeting we received. Our traveling party came alive."

On the following morning, Thursday, they visited the festival grounds. "Speechless would best describe the reaction of the group, the idea of having such a facility in a community was amazing," Finnegan added.

The fest really started for its Galway visitors that year, with what became a true traditional round of fun that included a reception followed by a wonderful night of entertainment. The relationship between Galway and Milwaukee was never the same after that first night. "We arrived, fell in love, bonded and a new baby was conceived, now known as the 'Spirit of Galway,'" Finnegan indicated.

Milwaukee Irish Fest is now on all calendars in Galway. Everyone knows about the festival and the people behind it, according to the broadcaster. "Each year, we bring a senior political figure with the group. They cannot believe the energy and entertainment. The festival is now more Irish than Ireland itself," he went on.

Finnegan's 10th year of involvement was in 2005. Each year, he has brought his family, starting when his children were toddlers. Over dinner in the spring of 2005, he asked the children which event they would prefer to attend that summer: Disneyland or Milwaukee Irish Fest. With disbelief and shock, he said that both exclaimed, "'Milwaukee, of course, to our friends.' I think that statement summarizes the festival."

Although Irish tourism official Anne Melia returns home exhausted from her forays to Milwaukee, she has always been appreciative of the response shown to her and the other Galwegians. Wisconsin's former Governor Tommy Thompson, who is an admitted lover of all things Irish, once invited the Galway group to the governor's mansion in Madison and they all developed great friendships.

From her booth, Melia regularly hands out approximately 2,000 packets of information and has occasionally run out of promotional materials due to the size of the crowds. When that occurs, Melia usually gives requesters the toll-free number at Tourism Ireland and the literature is sent to them from its warehouse.

Dealing with long hours is only a minor challenge because with the large group of willing workers attending from Ireland, everybody takes a turn at manning the stand. Subsequently, the Irish get to roam the grounds and take in the rest of the festival. For Melia, meeting with old friends also makes her visits to Milwaukee worthwhile. Many of the visitors lodge at the comfortable Milwaukee Athletic Club where, after each day's exhausting work, they head to the facility's third floor where there is usually "a grand sing-song" over relaxing beverages.

Paddy Maher, secretary of the Clare Tourist Council in 2003, promised continued support of the festival and indicated he had always "passed on the good word here in Co. Clare, both on radio and newspaper, about the Irish Fest." Friends told Bill McDonaugh of Galway Cottages about the festival, convincing him that he should have a presence there. That was in 1995 and he's been on hand ever since. Gerry Lowe, representing the Shannon region, was even delighted to begin losing his voice because of the amount of talking with potential visitors. Tanya Cathcart, marketing manager for the Fermanagh Lakelands Tourism Organization, was also excited about the level of interest in her area by Statesiders planning trips.

Helen Maguire, national consumer sales director for Aer Lingus, has been one of a progression of the airline's representatives to attend Irish Fest over the years. "This is a wonderfully fun event and a great way to reach our targets. I didn't realize the scale," she said during a break between a crush of questioners in 2004. Keeping a close watch over it all on behalf of Tourism Ireland, the official government tourism bureau, is Chicago-based Marie McKown. She is a fast-moving bundle of Celtic energy who knows the best way to traverse the Gap of Dunloe and booking the best B&Bs in Ballymaloe.

The British, representing Northern Ireland from their consulate in Chicago, have appreciated having a presence on

Irish Consul Charles Sheehan and Irish Ambassador Noel Fahey

Minister Sile de Valera

Irish Consul Frank Sheridan

Vice Consul Fionna Flood

Tanya Cathcart of Fermanagh Lakeland Tourism

Herbie Francis and Don Wilmont are proud of their
Causeway Coast and Glens

the grounds. Officials agreed that the festival exceeded any expectations they had, particularly with the size, the variety of offerings, numbers of visitors, the skillful organization and crowd management. In fact, many in the Windy City office who are Northern Irish or of Irish ancestry regularly include a Milwaukee visit in their summer plans.

Deputy Consul Michael W. Hewitt found Irish Fest a "very enjoyable experience" when he toured in 1992. Caroline Cracraft, vice consul for press and public affairs in the Chicago consulate, has attended since the early 1990s. In 2004, she brought along a very impressed Andy Pike, consul for Northern Ireland working out of the British consulate in New York.

Since the festival always ensured that there were performance groups from Northern Ireland and representatives from various regional tourist bureaus -- as well as local civic officials from cities like Larne with its Protestant majority population -- the British officials felt welcome in Irish America. In turn, they appreciated the opportunity to promote the attractions, businesses and culture of Northern Ireland.

There is an easy answer as to whether or not these British representatives were comfortable at the festival and if the presence of Northern Ireland's performers and vendors has been valuable. "Very much so," said Cracraft. "For us to be seen on the stage at the opening ceremonies and for us to be seen with our colleagues and senior visitors from the Republic -- often to the surprise of festgoers -- reinforces that we are all working to promote the arts and heritage and culture and handiwork of the whole island," she reiterated.

In 2005, she was joined by Andrew Seaton, the British consul general in Chicago; Nigel Hamilton, head of the Northern Ireland Civil Service and secretary to the Northern Ireland Executive; and Tim Losty, director of the Northern Ireland Bureau in Washington, D.C. While in the city, the contingent made contacts with business and artistic organizations to forge new and strengthen existing bonds between Wisconsin and Northern Ireland.

International Celtic links are solidified not only through visits by the Irish and Northern Irish, but also by reciprocal excursions which are valuable means of solidify working relationships with political, educational and cultural leaders and institutions. Irish Fest Director Jane Anderson regularly journeys to Ireland to meet with the counties interested in participating in Irish Fest, with meetings designed as orientations to the festival. "My goal is to tell everyone in Ireland about Irish Fest...one-by-one," she laughed.

However, it is very hard to tell people in Ireland about the size and scope of the festival, Anderson indicated. "Most are in awe when they arrive," she said, adding that the counties recognize that Irish Fest patrons are their target audience and that the event provides a good opportunity to promote travel to their areas. The festival is happy to make such information readily available to the festgoers.

Anderson first visited Ireland in 1992, subsequently making annual trips. She hits the ground running and covers many kilometers meandering through Ireland's glens and byways. She always travels to Dublin to meet with government representatives and then moves on to Galway, named Milwaukee's Irish sister city in 2001. From there, her travels vary, depending on the plans of each year's festival. Appointments are arranged in advance, but Anderson stays flexible because one meeting often leads to another introduction.

The relationship between Irish Fest and Ireland is unique among the nation's other festivals, a fact playing a large role in ensuring the quality of the event. The festival has also been the catalyst for the governments of Northern Ireland and the Republic of Ireland to work together on cross-border cultural activities such as the appearance of the Belfast Harp Orchestra in 1992.

Other Irish Fest board members, coordinators and volunteers have also visited Ireland, always receiving warm welcomes. The return on these relationships stemming from the trips has been tenfold. Festival visitors have had tea with the president of Ireland, chatted with prime ministers, sat in a session of the *Dáil Eireann* (Irish parliament) and attended special music performances.

From the beginning, fest volunteers were already abroad scouting out potential performers and exhibits that would be appropriate. In 1983, a busy Nancy Walczyk met with Michael Colgin, coordinator of the Dublin Theater Festival, representatives of the Irish Architectural Archives, author Brian de Breffny, Paul Hadfield of Theater Ireland and Kathleen White of the Ministry of Foreign Affairs. Milwaukee's own Dub City native John Gleeson was also always at the ready to provide important links with homeland officials.

Volunteer Tom Kennedy has been to Ireland three times: once with his wife, board member/fest president Colleen, once with their entire family to attend a wedding in Belfast and once with festival board member Pat Russell to the Galway Arts Festival. Kennedy indicated that it was "absolutely incredible" how many people stopped them on the street if they were wearing Irish Fest clothing to say, "I've been there" or "are you from Milwaukee?"

"It is a remarkable accomplishment to everyone involved in Irish Fest to know that we are truly a 'household' name in many parts of Ireland," he added.

Mike Brady visited Ireland In 1998, 1999 and 2000 with daughter Mara, a world champion dancer who was competing in the All-Ireland competitions. In Galway, Dingle, Sligo, Donegal, Clifden and Doolin, she and her Trinity friends demonstrated their high-kicking skills.

Everyone seemed to know about Irish Fest and the Bradys spotted festival bumper stickers from one end of the country to the other.

In 1995, Peg Hamill's cousin from Iowa, who was coming into town for the festival, asked if young Patrick Connolly -- a newly immigrated Irishman who was living in Iowa -- could stay with the Hamill clan for the weekend. He was willing to work on Bob Hamill's grounds crew in exchange for sleeping space on the family room floor. Connolly has returned to help at the festival every year since then. He has been interviewed several times from Milwaukee Irish Fest on the live Galway radio broadcast, with his family and friends listening intently every year from Ireland.

Now married, with identical twin sons, Connolly has become a part of the extended Hamill universe. His family has also hosted the Hamills three times on its lovely farm in Gort, near Galway. In 2004, most of the Hamills traveled to Iowa to reunite with most of Patrick's family visiting from Ireland. Ironically, both the Connolly and Hamill families have seven boys and three girls and their friendships, fostered through Irish Fest continue to be a blessing. "Our families are very similar. However, the Connollys say the evening rosary a lot faster than we do," asserted Peg Hamill.

The festival offers plenty of opportunities for the Irish to mix and mingle with their Celtic counterparts in Yankeeland. Waltons Music of Ireland became a mainstay of the Cultural Village and continues to present classes throughout the weekend. For Niall Walton, Waltons' managing director, the festival also provided a valuable forum from which to announce an annual Irish song scholarship. In 2001, Walton indicated that his firm would donate $1,000 for its "Sing an Irish Song" grant that would hopefully revitalize the Irish song tradition. The purpose of the award was to "encourage aspiring musicians, singers and songwriters to perform and create new Irish music and to strengthen and preserve Irish music in all its forms."

Niall Walton and his wife, Marie

Connections

Mary Pat Flanagan and Tommy Ryan, 1992

Spirit of Galway booth

Helen Maguire of Aer Lingus

Walton also took advantage of the Irish Fest bully pulpit to relaunch his firm's famous Glenside recording label. Glenside was initially started in 1951, issuing more than 350 different recordings. Many now-famous Irish artists such as Noel Purcell, Joe Lynch, Mary McGonigle, Delia Murphy, Charlie McGee and Brendan O'Reilly made early Glenside records. Many of the songs were broadcast on a radio program sponsored by the label, which was heard on Irish airwaves from 1952 to 1981. For many years, the broadcast was one of the few performing outlets for Irish songwriters and recording artists.

In another popular activity, the company has long hosted its March of the Bodhrans on the festival's final Sunday nights. Drummers walk from the firm's tent in the cultural area to the Aer Lingus stage for the Scattering, the last gathering of musicians where they can say their goodbyes.

The fest itself was "reality gone mad" according to Peadar O'Dowd, a fest guest in 2003, writing in the *Galway Now* magazine. "The whole of Irish heritage and culture was rolled out on a carpet of delight along the shoreline of Lake Michigan, described, appropriately, in the fest brochure, as 'Galway Bay.' Musical instruments, from bodhráns to harps, fiddles to bags of pipes, set a thousand feet tapping as the relentless sun looked over its shoulder and wondered what the hell was happening. *The Sound of Music* was never like this," he said.

Seanachie Batt Burns was a big help in spreading the word about Irish Fest. "From an entertainer's point of view, Milwaukee Irish Fest was always a dream. You were treated as a professional, everything was well-organized and the volunteers were extremely friendly and helpful. You felt that you were wanted and appreciated. The layout of the grounds was excellent," the storyteller exclaimed.

"Irish Fest is now recognized as a premier showcase of Irish tradition and culture. The promotion of the Irish language, the introduction of good theater, the exhibits were all great innovations and it was this approach and development that has contributed to its amazing success," Burns continued.

The storyteller, a former elementary school principal from the village of Sneem in Co. Kerry, used to perform for Shamrock clubs in many parts of Wisconsin in the early 1980s. He heard about Milwaukee from the late Gordon Reese, a staunch member of The Shamrock Club of Wisconsin-Madison and great supporter of Irish Fest. Reese made the contacts for Burns and since his recommendation carried weight, Burns was first booked in 1986. He attended many of the early Milwaukee fests and was again a featured performer in 2005.

Burns' fond memories of those early years include layovers at the Park East Hotel, where there "were rare nights of entertainment and carousing in that establishment. I think all of the entertainers loved that scene and there was wonderful camaraderie between entertainers and festival attendees."

Between 2001 and 2004, Galway bookseller Des Kenny has sold several thousand Irish-themed histories, novels, poetry, political treatises and related volumes from his expansive stall in the Cultural Area. He was concerned about his first appearance because he did not know anyone at the festival and worried that his books would have disappeared en route from Ireland. But when he arrived on the grounds, the boxes were all in place, much to his relief. "I couldn't get over that welcome," he said. Kenny also found time on his Milwaukee visits to scour the city's shops searching for used books to ship home for resale.

One of the most important places for the Irish to gather at the festival has always been around the Gaeltacht, one of John Gleeson's ideas, which was created in the late 1980s as part of the Cultural Area. Some of the volunteers there in the early days were Nancy Walczyk, Kathy Mallon, Kathy Radaj, Susan Radaj and Pat Smith. They handwrote hundreds of name tags in Irish for the festivalgoers, which was a challenge when it came to names like Kyle, Cody or Courtney. Mary June Hanrahan took over the area in 1994 and expanded its offerings. *Conradh na Gaeilge*, the Irish language organization in Milwaukee, continues to provide a team of informed volunteers who give lessons, sell books and provide great *craic*. Among them have been Sandy Hofmann, Seámas Kearney, Fr.. Peadar Ó Conghaile, Bruce Barr, Tomás McCormick, Lou Harper, Jack Mason, Joel Travis, Jill Baade, Kathleen Dineen, Eibhlín Carpenter and Mícheál Payne. Ina Kielly, Wendy Landvatter and Sinéad Pitterle are carrying on where Hanrahan left off.

The friendly clutter of tents, booths, displays, stages and sound equipment is reminiscent of a village in Connemara, encouraging Old Ireland to mix with the new. Amid the flow of mellifluous voices, fluent and just-beginning Irish speakers find friends with whom they can mingle, laugh and work on diction. Liam Ó Cuinneagáin, director of Oideas Gael, Glencolumcille, Co. Donegal, and now chairman of *Uduras na Gaeltachta*, the Gaeltacht authority in Ireland, was instrumental in providing an understanding of the importance of the Irish language, with Gleeson a constant source of inspiration, information and ideas. As Mary June Hanrahan recalled, Gleeson taught the first volunteers words like *Oireachtas*, which is an important yearly competition and celebration of the Irish culture back "home."

The Gaeltacht area continues to attract organizations in Ireland such as *Foras na Gaeilge*, which sent representatives Caitlín Ní Chonghaile and Áine Seoighe for a number of years. Maitias Mac Cárthaigh with *Fios Feasa* and *Gael Saoire* with Steve O Cúláin and Bertie Feeney have also attended.

Boston's Bridget Fitzgerald, a Connemara-born singer was another early guest. Chicago musician Pat Cloonan, an accordion player born in Co. Galway, helps make the Gaeltacht a meeting place for numerous native Irish from Chicago such as Aine Meenaghan, Kevin Henry and Tim O'Sullivan. Many advocates for the Irish language have come

from Madison. Dineen Grow, one of the organizers of Madison's Celtic Cultural Center, has lectured a number of times.

Other guests from Ireland have enriched the festival and visitors' lives with wit, fun and comradeship, Hanrahan pointed out. She named a few: Roisín White, Gearóid Ó hAllmhuráin, Ray MacMánais, Tim Denneny, Geaóid Mordha, Eamon ÓDonnachadha, James Flannagan and Meaití Jó Shéamuis, "who has taken us to the Irish Gaeltacht with his radio shows direct to Ireland on *Raidió na Gaeltachta*." One of the more distinguished guests was Tomas O'Canainn, honored as Ard Ollamn, Supreme Bard of the *Fleadh Cheoil* for 2004.

The Gaeltacht receives rave reviews from its Irish visitors. After one visit, poet Mary O'Mally of Galway said that "in the cultural village at the quiet end of the grounds, the Gaeltacht tent is perhaps the closest to home in terms of atmosphere. An array of artists sing, dance and play with humor and grace. The audience listens, chats and laughs."

GaelSaoire's Bertie O Finneadha (Feeney) indicated that a good motto for the festival might be "that nothing is a problem." As such, Irish Fest should continue to go from strength to strength, he emphasized. His optimistic outlook was based on the fact that "I never encountered any problem that wasn't amicably solved with the utmost of cooperation," he pointed out. Feeney first started coming to Milwaukee in 1998 with the Spirit of Galway group to promote business links, particularly in the tourism sector, as well as for the fun and *craic* everyone has meeting friends each year.

"As we say in Irish, '*Níl neart go cur le chéile & go mairfidh muid uilig an 100*." The phrase, meaning "there's strength in numbers and may we all live to 100," could well be a festival motto.

Francis McPeake, Tomas O'Canainn of University College Cork, Harry Bradshaw of RTÉ and Paddy Clark share a discussion on music

Chapter 9

The "grandfather" of Irish Fest and namesake of the festival's archives, John J. Ward, Jr., demonstrates his musical ability

Saving the Past

Archives

Saving the Past
Archives

"We named the archives after my dad and also established it in honor of my mother."

Ed Ward, founder of Milwaukee Irish Fest,
speaking of his parents John and Jane (Cagney)

Almost everything regarding Irish music can be found in the second-floor archives of the Irish Fest Center in Wauwatosa. The only things that seem to be missing amid the artifacts are 76 trombones and McNamara's band. That notwithstanding, enjoying a comfortable home at the center is one of the world's largest collections of Celtic sound: the John J. Ward, Jr., Irish Music Archives, established by Milwaukee Irish Fest in 1992.

"There was always music in our family," said Ed Ward, founder of Irish Fest. Looking back at his growing-up days in the Chicago area and in Kenosha, Wisconsin, he recalled, "My dad's sister, Eileen Ward Fitzgerald, and her kids had a group. At family parties, we would all end up doing something with music."

Jim Vint and Harry Bradshaw

Ward's interest in music was also sparked by his grandfather, John Ward, who had published five books on Irish music. While traveling in Dublin in 1991, the younger Ward visited the Irish Traditional Music Archives. "I was going through music books on the shelves and came across copies of my grandfather's collections," he said. "Recognizing that these books, which were part of our family's heritage, had historical significance and value, made me wonder where a record of Irish America's musical heritage was being preserved."

Since no significant collection existed, Ward decided that Milwaukee's Irish Fest might be a natural place to preserve and protect this music and music-related items. At first, the Archives consisted of a small collection of tapes. Offering free tickets to Irish Fest in exchange for donations spurred the collection's growth.

Barry Stapleton, with Irish rocker and music historian Ian Whitcomb and Ed Ward

In addition to receiving gifts from the public and from entertainers, the Archives tries to document as much as the staff and volunteers can during the festival. Photographer John Alley shoots from 20 to 30 rolls of film on the entertainers, becoming good friends with many of them over the years. Dave Sargeant and Michael O'Regan videotape numerous

Bob Burke

Dave Sargeant

over the years. Dave Sargeant and Michael O'Regan videotape numerous performances. Stage managers save items signed by the bands to preserve and to commemorate the history of the festival.

The collection, now considered the largest outside Ireland, is estimated at around 40,000 items, the majority of which are recordings. In 2004, the Archives had 4,000 CDs, 5,000 LPs, 5,000 to 6,000 78-rpm records and 4,000 pieces of sheet music. In addition, there are still-to-be-counted tapes, posters, cylinders, Victrolas, instruments, ads, concert brochures and tickets, plus dozens of files on Irish entertainers. The shelves are packed with 2,000 books, ranging from biographies of performers of such stature as Bing Crosby, George M. Cohan and Victor Herbert to the *American Dance Band & Discography, 1917-1942*, and George Dennis Zimmerman's *Songs of Irish Rebellion*.

"In the beginning, we took everything," said archivist Barry Stapleton, as he looked over the shelves and display cases packed with material. "But now that our collections have grown, we're focused on specific items," he said.

Among the recent acquisitions in late 2004 were several beautiful old Irish music books donated by Milwaukeean Tom O'Connell, who brought them back from Ireland. One of O'Connell's friends, Noel Lonergan, presented the gifts to him when hearing about the Archives. Two of the books are collections of dance tunes, one of which was published in Dublin in 1911 and the other in Glasgow probably around the same time.

A Bing Crosby scrapbook donated by Tim O'Brien of Milwaukee was another major

acquisition. O'Brien's mother, Dolores Lillian O'Brien, was a huge Crosby fan and collected many articles about the singer between the 1930s and 1950s.

The largest single gathering of material is considered the general "Irish Fest Collection." Every year, the festival gets over 500 applications from bands wanting to play the fest. So these CDs and public relations packs eventually go into the Archives. All other donations also go into this collection, plus any purchases made of special materials.

The first major donation -- and the second largest in terms of artifacts -- consisted of the Michael and Mary Comer Collection which amounted to almost 5,000 items. The collection, donated to Irish Fest in May, 1998, contains reel-to-reel tapes, CDs, cassettes, 45-rpm and 78-rpm records. Most of the materials are on Irish labels, collected in Ireland by Michael Comer, whose radio show *Echoes of Erin* ran for more than 25 years in Cleveland, Ohio. Pieces date from the 1940s through the 1980s, with a strong focus on 1960s and 1970s record albums. Most of these artifacts would be very difficult to find today.

The collection also contains more than 30 pieces of recording and playback equipment used by Comer in his basement studio. Several dozen of the Ohio broadcaster's commendations and award plaques were included in the move to Milwaukee.

Dave Sargeant, a retired television engineer from Miami who first visited Irish Fest in 1992, helped organize the Comer collection. Around 1995, he started taking photographs at the Summer School and the fest and giving

them to the Archives. Through those donations, he met various festival officials who asked if he could help them decide what of Comer's equipment might be of use to the Archives. He was delighted to donate his time for a few weeks each year to design and build a re-recording facility in the back room at the Archives. Since then, he has added improvements to the facility. Around 2001, Sargeant began videotaping Summer School classes and festival performances for archival purposes.

Stapleton secures permissions from the performers for the tapings, indicating they are only for the festival's files. Recordings are done with a single camera, sometimes simply locked down on a cover shot with no attempt to make a production from it. Although the public may be able to view such recordings at the Archives, no copies may be made and taken away.

In 2003, *The Irish American Post* presented another major collection, consisting of 700 tapes and CDs of contemporary and commercial Irish music. Many of the artists had been interviewed and their music reviewed in the now on-line publication which has been covering the international Irish music scene since 1991.

The Ed and Cathy Ward Collection, with a base of 400-plus LPs, CDs and cassettes that Ward had collected since the 1970s, is also housed in the Archives. In the late 1970s, Ward and his brother, Chuck, operated Irish Music Ltd., which distributed for numerous Irish recording labels. Operating in the initial years of Green Linnet and Shanachie, Ward was able to collect many of these firms' earliest releases. More recently, Ward focused on acquiring items that would complement the Comer Collection. He subsequently has assembled more than 1,000 pieces of Irish sheet music, several thousand Irish and Irish-American 45-rpm and 78-rpm records, hundreds of song books and music periodicals and a number of antique phonographs and juke boxes.

There are also several other well-documented, themed bodies of work in the archives. Irish Fest's John McCormack collection is one of the world's largest assemblages of this great Irish tenor's recordings, including 12 rare cylinders dating from 1903 and 1904. Considered the gems of the Irish Fest collection,

Archives Photographer John Alley

Barry Stapleton directs the ceremony inaugurating the Archives' Hall of History in 2003

Marquette Stankowski Family and Kathy Crosby

the artifacts were purchased from Neil Corning, a collector on the East Coast who was eager to sell them.

Fortunately, a McCormack sponsor was found in Michael (Mr. Mike) Corenthal of Milwaukee's Yesterday's Memories shop who helped pull off the deal. The collection also has advertisements, books, postcards, more than 40 photographs and over 50 LPs. McCormack's 78-rpm records were produced on Odeon, Columbia, Regal, Okeh, Gramophone G&T, HMV and Victor labels. Corenthal is also interested in Jewish-Irish material from the turn of the century.

Through the efforts of archivist Stapleton, the Bing Crosby Collection is the largest public collection of the noted crooner's recordings outside of Gonzaga University in Spokane, Washington. The famed singer graduated from Gonzaga High School in 1920, receiving an honorary doctorate from the university in 1937. Most of the Irish Fest collection was donated by Crosby fans across the United States who contributed recordings, books, photos and Crosby memorabilia.

There are several other important collections. Jerry Kelly of Philadelphia was an avid collector of Irish music. Upon his death, more than 1,000 of his LPs and cassettes were given to Irish entertainer Seamus Kennedy who subsequently donated the collection. In addition, Fest volunteer Bob Burke has contributed a massive amount of Irish film material.

Burke set up a display in the festival's Cultural Area in 1994, using 24 display boards to cover the history of film and show how the Irish were involved or portrayed. His holdings included movies from America, Ireland and other parts of the world. More than 100 films were represented with posters, stills, lobby cards, magazines, photographs and newspaper clippings. A special tribute to Irish-American director John Ford was included because it was the centennial celebration of his birth that year. To help in preparing the display, Burke even attended a conference in New York City that covered Irish film. Despite a rainstorm that threatened his treasures, the display received rave reviews and much media coverage. "It was a moment in the spotlight never known before," Burke admitted proudly.

Burke continues to help at the Archives, despite now living in Dixon, Illinois, after his retirement from the United States Postal Service. Irish Fest acquired 3,000 books on Irish themes from Burke in 2004. His assignment is now to catalog numerous pieces of sheet music.

The Archives staff continues to seek material, especially that by Irish Americans of significant musical importance such as Chauncey Olcott, George M. Cohan, Rosemary Clooney and Patrick Gilmore. "Any items associated with these performers and many others of their stature will help us document their lives and legacies," said Stapleton.

Faced with the daunting task of figuring out how to track all these offerings, volunteers have developed their own easily trackable catalog system. Items are first assessed and cataloged, with their details scanned into a computer program. If necessary, they are placed in protective coverings.

As with all Irish Fest tasks, a large coterie of volunteers aids Stapleton. Jim Vint acts as the primary technical assistant, with Bernie Beutner doing the majority of catalog input. Betty Mikush helps with cleaning the recordings and, along with her husband, Ed, performs numerous other tasks in keeping the Archives humming. Tom O'Connell handles entertainment files. Cyndy Beecroft coordinates the Archives tent at Irish Fest and puts out an Archives newsletter. Bob Harrold, Marianne Fisher, Dave Wesolowski, Dick Faherty, Mike Kenny and many others also help out.

In addition to the Comer audio studio, the office uses three computers, a video station and a large scanner that accommodate most of the facility's technical needs.

Archivist Stapleton has been involved with the Irish community since the 1970s, including serving as an officer in the Shamrock Club. He became active with Irish Fest in the middle 1980s, acting as a stage manager and eventually an assistant music coordinator. "I've always had an interest in music and history, so this position was a natural progression for me when Ed (Ward) informed me about it in 1992," he said.

Along with visiting many other Archives and museums to see how displays were arranged and items collected and cataloged, Stapleton attends seminars and conferences focusing on preserving music. For instance, in 2004, he attended the John McCormack Conference in London. Irish Fest also belongs to several preservation and archival organizations, such as the Association for Recorded Sound Collections and the Society for Ethnomusicology, that help keep him up-to-date on the profession's technicalities.

On a typical day, Stapleton begins work answering the e-mail inquiries in the morning and organizing tasks or projects for any volunteers who may be coming in to help. In 2004 and early 2005, he worked hard on

music through any Australian music stores or through other institutions, the man contacted the Archives. Stapleton was able to find the correct score and send it along.

Contacting entertainers and securing contracts for the festival's rock stage takes up some of Stapleton's time in the winter and spring. In the summers, he goes on the road with exhibits, which have become a major part of Irish Fest's educational thrust. The exhibits generally feature 100 poster-sized panels that depict a certain artist such as Bing Crosby, John McCormack or George M. Cohan. Displays may also focus on an era or theme such as Irish rock music or Tin Pan Alley.

The Archives also provides lectures, videos and listening stations to support each exhibit. Stapleton is regularly on the road, giving up to 10 talks every year, and visits three to four other Irish fests around the country with his displays. "As we put programs together, we hope to bring them to as many people as possible, especially colleges," he indicated.

developing the festival's eagerly anticipated 25th anniversary CD project. "I thoroughly enjoy learning about some obscure Irish American who may have had an impact on our cultural heritage. It's also very gratifying finding new musicians," he said.

Stapleton also helps on more esoteric projects. In 2005, he assisted a man in Australia seeking the sheet music for *Two Shillelagh O'Sullivan*, a song by Bing Crosby. The Australian planned to sing the tune for his father, confined to a care center because of cancer. Having a difficult time finding the

In addition to his own research, Stapleton solicits information from experts on particular subjects. For a Bing Crosby exhibit, he solicited little-known details about the singer from the Crosby family and major Crosby scholars and historians, such as *Village Voice* music critic Gary Giddins, who wrote the critically acclaimed *Bing Crosby: A Pocketful of Dreams: The Early Years, 1903-1940,* and well-known historian/collector Greg Van Beek.

Stapleton and the staff routinely invite touring musicians to visit and spread the word about the collections. Fiddler Frankie Gavin of De Danann and Mrs. Bing Crosby have been

Lectures by notable historians and music personalities are a big part of activities at the Irish Fest Center

among the notables perusing the Archives to look over the offerings and leave memorabilia. Others have included Liam Clancy, squeezebox impresario Joe Burke and tin whistle whiz and flutist Joanie Madden of Cherish the Ladies. Seamus Connolly, of Killaloe, Co. Clare, who is director of Boston College's Irish Studies Music, Song and Dance Program, has also visited the facility. Escorting songwriter Barry McGuire was another big thrill for Stapleton, as were stops by Éamon Ó Cuív and Sile de Valera, ministers of Ireland's Department of Arts, Heritage, Gaeltacht and the Islands.

Working with other festivals and institutions, community centers and universities is another way the Archives supports its mission. The archives collaborated with New York University and Professor Mick Moloney in putting together the exhibit on Irish American song stories and Tin Pan Alley. The display originally used material from Moloney's personal collection and was exhibited at NYU's Glucksman Ireland House. The Archives expanded the exhibit in 2004. The Archives is also collaborating with the Library of Congress for an exhibit scheduled to open in March, 2008.

A "Hall of History" was introduced in 2003 to show off some of its major holdings. The numerous artifacts highlighted in a long hallway adjacent to the archives on the Irish Fest Center's second floor have been very well-received, according to Stapleton.

Even with the expanding number of donations, Stapleton doesn't feel that the Archives will run out of space soon. He sees the challenge as a question of organization. "The Archives has a lifetime of work remaining. We'll only be the beginning," he emphasized.

Stapleton is hoping to publish a book within the next few years which will go a long way in disseminating some of the information learned over the past few years. In a high point of her Milwaukee visit in 2005, Irish President Mary McAleese toured the archives. She spent almost an hour looking over the collection and admiring the array of material.

The elder Mr. Ward should be pleased.

Cyndy Beecroft and volunteers staff the Archives exhibit at Irish Fest

The 6,000-piece collection from Cleveland's Michael Comer overflows the Archives

Barry Stapleton looks over an exhibit on the Hall of History

Chapter 10

Irish President Mary McAleese visits the *Gaeltacht* area in the Cultural Village

Sharing the Gold

Impact

Sharing the Gold

"One of the things that sets Irish Fest apart from all the other Irish festivals in the United States and abroad is its expansive vision. There is a place for simply every kind of Irish and Irish American form of cultural expression in the festival. This underlies a generosity of spirit and tolerance for diversity that is rare in public arts performance in this country at a time when the arts are more compartmentalized than they have ever been.

"For the visitor and even for myself as an artist after coming to the festival over the past 25 years, it is almost impossible to process the scale and scope of this mighty event...I have been at every major Irish festival in the U.S. over the past few decades and I can attest that there simply has never been anything even close to the breadth and scale of the Milwaukee Irish Fest."

Mick Moloney, musicologist/historian/author/musician

Dancers promote an early Irish Fest at City Hall

The late Mayor Henry W. Maier, the Founding Father of Milwaukee's Festivals who originated the concept of Summerfest and the City of Festivals parades, was always a fan of Irish Fest. In the spring of 1981, he happily signed a proclamation kicking off the first Irish music and culture weekend.

Maier, in office from 1960 to 1988, also regularly received letters from out-of-towners praising the Green-tinged extravaganza. He always responded to those notes. Maier cheerily replied to one family from Northbrook, Illinois, who lauded the fest in 1984, "We are all absolutely delighted that you had such a great time, and we're glad to know that you may be able to spend more time with us next year. See you at next year's fest, and best wishes to you all!" Hizzoner, the mayor, exclaimed.

A Common Council proclamation (File Number 84-720)

advanced by then-Alderman Wayne Frank on July 20, 1984, also expressed the city's enthusiastic appreciation for what the fest had already accomplished.

But why is Milwaukee so successful as a host city for the world's largest Irish cultural event? It certainly is not because of a large Irish population, according to local historian Tom Cannon. "With only 5.75 percent of the population of the state claiming to be of Irish ancestry according to the 1990 census, Wisconsin is only 28th in size of Irish population among all the states," he pointed out.

Wisconsin contains only 1.2 percent of the nation's 22.7 million Americans claiming Irish ancestry, Cannon said, adding that Boston, Chicago and New York have much larger Irish populations than Milwaukee. "Milwaukee County had only five percent of its population in 1990 listed as Irish," Cannon recounted.

Resolved, That the Common Council of the City of Milwaukee herewith congratulates the ambitious and enthusiastic organizers of Irish Fest for the successful culmination of their efforts in family entertainment on August 17, 18 and 19, 1984; and be it Further Resolved, That the Common Council of the City of Milwaukee does hereby officially recognize Irish Fest as a splendid civic event of benefit to the entire community, and is pleased to sponsor and endorse Irish Fest, in addition to commending those public spirited citizens who have worked so diligently to bring Milwaukee this premier summertime event...

Festival folks deliver the raffle gold

Mary Clancy, wife of the late singer Paddy Clancy, adds materials to the Archives

Jennifer Studebaker and Marci Pelzer

Cory Rice and Trish Quasney of Todd Robert Murphy Advertising and Public Relations, 1996

So what *were* the reasons. The answer to "Why Milwaukee" was not numbers, but it was cohesion, Cannon emphasized. Cohesion of size, of geography and of connection. The Irish population in Milwaukee and Milwaukee County had been originally concentrated in the "old Third Ward" immediately south of the downtown. This concentration moved to the near west side of the city in the Merrill Park neighborhood. Over time, the population dispersed throughout the city but generally to the West. Milwaukee is a city where there may only be "two degrees of separation" and the resulting links and networks are very strong. Because the population was small, there were only a few Irish organizations like the Shamrock Club of Wisconsin in the 1980s. Subsequently, receiving the Irish community's support and getting out the message to the public was thus relatively simple.

Cannon went on to say that this cohesion and the vision of festival founder Ed Ward are the obvious keys to "Why Milwaukee?" Ward was able to articulate that vision and dream of an Irish renaissance and, because of the cohesiveness of the Irish "connections," his dream rippled across many circles, Cannon indicated. These circles connected with others and drew in multiple groups of people who wanted to participate and help build the vision. The dream of the Irish community in Milwaukee was to have a festival that celebrated the heart of the Irish experience as expressed through the mist of time, history, legend, storytelling and music and to bring that experience to a new generation, he concluded.

In addition, the festival has been duly chronicled by massive media coverage over the course of 25 years. All corners of the Celtic -- and non-Irish -- world have picked up on the event. The word has been spread not just with advertising but by articles in local and international publications. *Irish Music Magazine, Irish American News, The Irish American Post, Irish Times, Belfast News* and others in the observant world of ethnic media readily tune in to the festival's expansive potential. In addition, listeners hear of the fun firsthand by reports from the grounds by Galway Bay FM, Gaelic-language stations, *Radio Telefís Éireann* and Stateside broadcast reports.

Moving beyond tried-and-true entertainer interviews and concert reviews, Irish Fest has rightly earned a reputation for creating nontraditional marketing events that also garner attention and help bolster attendance.

Among them: painting green stripes down Chicago Street to the entrance gates; Paddy and Molly McFest visiting the State Capitol; planting an oversize Gulliver on the lakefront; and encouraging Milwaukee Institute of Art and Design students to compete for the annual poster design. The media has long realized that covering the Irish Fest story results in numerous nontraditional stories with which to regale readers, listeners and viewers.

Demonstrating the high quality of its creative support staff, the festival's marketing programs and its print materials have earned awards from the International Festivals Association and similar trade organizations. Working hard to get out the word started with Hintz & Company (1980-1994) and moved on to Todd Robert Murphy Advertising and

Public Relations (1995-1999), Bottom Line Marketing and Public Relations (2000); Stephan & Brady (2001); Versant Solutions (2002); and Marci Pelzer and Jennifer Studebaker (2003-2005)

Yet in order for the festival's public relations contractors to suggest good stories to the media, there must be an excellent product to pitch. Irish Fest's mission of promoting the Irish culture ensures that. Festival director Jane Anderson always revisits that goal when making decisions. Yet she admitted that even within the four days of the fest, the event still can't be all things for all people. But everyone involved tries hard to provide a cultural experience to the audience in whatever form it chooses to see and experience the fest, whether in listening to music, shopping or touring cultural displays.

Sometimes even goofiness pays off. To promote the raffle prizes and the pot of gold, Sandy Wright Hintz and her firm once developed a media event consisting of the Iroquois tour boat berthing on the Milwaukee River in downtown, carrying costumed characters and Paddy and Molly McFest. A pony cart awaited to transport the McFests and a pot of gold to the bank which had supplied the gold bullion and security. All was ready, including the three television stations, the local newspapers and radio.

After the boat arrived and the cameras started filming, the gold was dutifully placed on the back of the cart. The weight of the treasure and the McFests' girth resulted in the pony being lifted up off its feet and causing Paddy and Molly to tumble from their perch, along with the gold which scattered on the ground. No one was hurt, everyone roared with laughter and the event made all the news.

In another promo, the rotund Paddy, played by Mike Brady, was sent to the downtown YMCA to "work off" a few of the original pounds that puppetmaker Robin Reed had placed on him when first constructed. Paddy/Mike rode a stationary bicycle, performed aerobics and waddled laps to work up a good sweat. During his next appearance, a more svelte Paddy -- actually due to some nip and tuck tailoring -- greeted his fans. Photos of "work-out Paddy" were widely disseminated by the Y.

Staying open to innovative ideas and encouraging change are also necessary, even if the process involves attempting something new and perhaps failing. Some of the ideas were big and had a major impact. Others were smaller and had a minor impact. But they added up to a culture where new ideas were constantly encouraged, if not always implemented. This open-minded milieu keeps the festival on the leading edge of its market niche. Subsequently, it could be said that the fest's greatest success is the fact that it has indeed stayed fresh for 25 years.

There are several reasons that the festival remains on the cutting edge. First, the many infrastructure improvements on the grounds allowed the fest to physically expand to accommodate additional attractions. Milwaukee became a center of the Irish Renaissance because it had the perfect physical setting for a festival: the Henry Maier Festival Park on the shore of Lake Michigan. This beautiful locale, one built to accommodate festivals, was used by the Irish in ways that hadn't

Pat Russell painting a green stripe on Chicago Street

Irish Float, City of Festivals Parade

The Impact

125

Gulliver visits Milwaukee

been envisioned by others. For instance, Irish Fest was the first festival to have daily parades through the grounds and the first to use the adjacent Urban Park for related sports events such as hurling and Gaelic football.

Secondly, the festival's organizational structure has also been revamped many times to keep up with growing responsibilities. By 2005, the board numbered 18, with 125 coordinators and supervisors working year-round on their areas of interest. The fest also has a staff of four -- three full-time and one part-time -- and a clutch of dependable office volunteers. These talented board members and coordinators have been recruited from the city's business and government sectors. In Milwaukee, many fest volunteers of Irish descent comprise the management levels of numerous companies and organizations. They understood how to manage an organization to succeed.

Third, the festival has established a foundation, archives, a music school and scholarship programs. It is important to note that with such outreach, the individuals within the organization have remained committed to their original mission. While those activities outside the festival proper may be more broad than in the early years, they remain entirely consistent with what the early planners intended.

Fourth, with the purchase of the Irish Fest Center in Wauwatosa, the fest has a permanent, centralized location for its operations and a place to host additional endeavors. These range from holiday breakfasts with Nick McFest, a jocular distant "relative" of mascot Paddy, to lectures by visiting Irish scholars.

At the base of it all is the knowledge that audiences have become very sophisticated in understanding Irish music and culture. Subsequently, they always seek ever-expanding frontiers of fun and excitement. "We have reached out to draw in new audiences by developing new themes each year, building new exhibits, changing the line-up even when that wasn't the popular thing to do with some fans, hosting the Hootenanny and introducing the Rock Stage," director Anderson pointed out.

Regardless of their reasons for attending, patrons have often said that they plan their vacations around the third weekend in August so they can get their annual Celtic fix. A 1999 study commissioned by the Greater Milwaukee Convention & Visitors Bureau indicated 80 percent of fest-goers had attended in prior years, demonstrating a very high rate of return.

For a number of years, Irish Fest conducted its own survey during the festival. Of all the festivals, including Summerfest, Irish Fest has the largest percentage of out-of-town visitors. The percentage of non-metro visitors is over 50 percent. Many people make this their vacation destination and book rooms a year in advance. This high non-metro attendance is almost like insurance for bad weather periods. Guests from out of town would rather sing in the rain at Irish Fest than spend time in their hotel rooms. The festival grounds now have enough covered spaces that allow patrons to get out of the rain for brief periods as well. The number of patrons coming from Chicago and northern Illinois is so great that the directions to the festival for them are simply:

"Follow all the Illinois license plates with stickers that say 'Thank God I'm Irish'."

The festival has had an impact on the Milwaukee economy. It is virtually impossible to find a hotel room in the metro area the weekend of Irish Fest. Visitors are directed to locations 20 to 40 miles away to find a room.

The flood of visitors also impacts the movement of traffic in downtown Milwaukee and its surface streets, particularly near the freeway's ramps. One helpful way of alleviating some of the vehicular congestion has been the Milwaukee County Transit System's shuttle bus program, accommodating Irish Fest visitors as early as 1982. The company's figures indicate that from 15,000 to 20,000 riders per weekend utilize this service, placing Irish Fest at the top of all the ethnic festivals in this regard. The service begins a half-hour before the gates open and runs up to a half-hour after they close. Tickets are $2 for a round trip to a downtown location and $5 for a freeway flier, with the latter program beginning in the late 1990s with the assistance of a federal grant.

Irish Fest has also been a pivotal supporter of the transit system's traditional St. Patrick's Day free-ride program, which begins at 6 p.m. on the High Holy Day and runs through the end of regularly scheduled service. In 1994, Miller Brewing Company approached the transit operators, suggesting an expansion of its sponsorship of a popular free-ride program held on New Year's Eve. The festival was enlisted to encourage support for the St. Patrick's project and did so by providing entertainers and Paddy McFest for kickoff ceremonies. Many festival volunteers also attended such marketing special events held the first five years of the service. Well-ingrained in the 'partygoers' mindsets on every March 17 since then, approximately 450,000 persons have taken advantage of the rides since they were launched.

Organizers and volunteers celebrated when the fest reached 100,000 in attendance in 1995. While that figure was never really considered a goal -- instead focusing on delivering a quality presentation and ensuring that people who came, stayed -- admittedly it was always in the back of everyone's minds that it would be grand to reach six-digits worth of visitors.

Fest management and volunteers visit other Irish festivals around the country during the year and attend Irish activities and concerts locally and abroad. As such, the relationships and friendships developed over the years have provided a lot of support. The festival has mentored organizations wishing to establish similar events in Ohio, the Twin Cities, Kansas City, Dallas and other communities.

In 1984, a contingent of Milwaukee volunteers journeyed to the Boston area to assist in setting up an Irish blowout in Foxboro's Sullivan Stadium. That mini-fest ultimately drew 20,000 fans and resulted in no end of hilarious stories related by those who experienced the offbeat expedition. The Milwaukeeans set up booths, ensured that performers made it to the stages, assisted with ticket taking and generally utilized their organizational expertise in multitudinous ways on behalf of the Beantowners. In 1997 and 2005, the fest also hosted spring Gathering Conferences, with workshops and lectures that attracted Irish-festival directors and coordinators from around the country.

Such linkages did not go without notice. "Irish Fest in Milwaukee is a strong example of what can be done in a communal sense. What I'm deeply proud of was the council that was held in Milwaukee to bring together festival coordinators throughout the country and what could be done in organizing, vending and cultural events for the fests. It has done a lot for the Irish festivals in the Midwest," Irish Consul General Frank Sheridan told reporter Joseph Moran of *The Irish American Post* in 1998.

For Athlone-born John O'Brien, chairman of the Cleveland Irish Fest -- launched three years after the Milwaukee venue began -- the opportunity to meet other fest management and exchange ideas was a marvelous idea. "We all get along just fine. When something comes up, we can just call each other," agreed O'Brien, who has attended Milwaukee's festival more than 10 times. A number of Milwaukeeans even volunteer for the Ohio event and vice versa.

Irish Fest can be therapeutic, as well. Francis (Red) Kennedy, of Springfield, Nebraska, has been coming to Milwaukee since 1982 to revel in the music and culture. For a number of years, he and wife Maggie would stay for a couple of days to help in teardown. In 1997, he showed up at the gates five weeks after a triple heart bypass. "I got well at the festival, it

Martin Hintz and Liam Clancy

From Celtic Women to...

"Celtic Women International was invited to participate at Irish Fest in the Sunday service for peace and reconciliation by marching in as a group, beginning in 1999. Its members have joined in this activity every year since then. As founder of Celtic Women International, I have been honored to be included in events at Irish Fest where dignitaries from Ireland are introduced at receptions of local people who are active in the Irish community.

"Because my interest was sparked at Irish Fest and carried over to the Celtic Women's conferences, I have been privileged to meet, and cause to visit Milwaukee, such Irish women as Morgan Llywelyn, Alice Taylor, Meda Ryan, Fiona Flood, Mary McGonigle, Freida Kelly, The Poor Clares and Maggie Cronin. These experiences have enriched my life."

Jean Bills, Tea Room volunteer

...Cultural Exhibits

"From working with Irish Fest, I've gained a sense of belonging...(and) a sense that I have created something of worth for lots of people. My face on television. My voice broadcast back to Ireland. Lots of friendships, both in Milwaukee and across the globe. Lots of sleep deprivation. And, oh, that I don't drink beer, the occasional shots of whiskey.

"I also seem to have developed a credence in terms of what I do. From dealing with government officials to university professors to artisans and artists, as a result of working at the festival in general and in the Cultural Area in particular, I have a currency...because of the festival. Of course, I have had to learn a lot about a lot of things. But I am able to go into a room, speak with folks and be able to sustain an intelligent conversation."

Brian Witt, Cultural Exhibits co-coordinator

Irish Fest Columbia Hospital Run

was the best cure-all. It got my good spirits back," he laughed. "Coming to Irish Fest is like going to heaven, Irish heaven."

Most performers are positive about what they say regarding Milwaukee Irish Fest, often telling how it impacted their careers. The entertainers continue to be impressed with the vastness of the festival, the number of volunteers, the organization and the fun. For Celtic impresario Tommy Makem, Irish Fest is "the premier Irish cultural festival in North America, and indeed, many -- myself included -- would say, the world."

Seanachie Batt Burns said that he found the audiences terrific. "My type of entertainment was very much the old humorous traditional storytelling and yarns. Many of the audiences comprised of people who had emigrated from Ireland in the 1960s and I suppose I struck a chord with them that brought them back many years," he indicated. "Irish Fest played a significant part in the advancement of my entertainment career in the United States. It looked good on the resume that you had performed in Milwaukee. It has been my biggest venue and has produced my best audiences."

There are amazing on-stage moments, too, that affect both the crowds and entertainers. On the last night of the 2003 festival, brothers Donal and Angus Leahy of the hard-driving Canadian family band, Leahy, joined The Clumsy Lovers for several songs, sitting down at the edge of the stage almost within touching distance of the cheering audience. "It was magical for us and I think for the audience," agreed the Lovers' Chris Jonat.

Magic occurs out of the spotlight, too. "Ever since I heard that Tom Rowe of Schooner Fare died, I've been haunted by the memory of a day I went to their room at the Park East," said Liam Clancy. "They were putting the final touches to a new song for the evening show. In the small hotel room, they gave full rein to 'Portland Town.' At one point in the song, they suddenly stopped playing the instruments and, *a cappella*, broke into a soaring harmony on the lines 'I see the light across the bay.' I broke out in goose bumps and tears welled up in my eyes. It was an overwhelming moment which I'll not forget," he said. "It was definitely one of the great moments in my Irish Fest experiences."

Over the past quarter-century, the fest has also provided a venue for out-of-the-ordinary musicians, encouraging the patrons to stretch their acceptance of the nontraditional. Martina Goggin of Galway's Dordán pointed out her band's music was not the typical sound associated with Irish music. "But the response we got from those who attended our concerts was very positive and most encouraging and certainly affirms our view that there is room for all types, and variations of Irish traditional music," she said.

Linda Rutherford of Celtic Fire wanted to say what a pleasure it was to play at the festival. "We were commenting to ourselves about the organization and professionalism of the whole staff. Tremendous crowds, tremendous venue, tremendous people....it's a real credit to your group," she indicated. Sarah Allen and Flook thanked the fest for having them perform. "You made us feel very welcome. We had a

The Impact

128

fantastic weekend of music-making and fun," she said, praising their volunteer driver for fetching the group from the airport and keeping them sane, thanking Jeanne Cissne for her constant, calm presence at the hotel front desk and praising all the crew at the Old Style stage for its support.

Mike Reynolds, on the committee coordinating the Omagh Community Youth Choir, was enthusiastic after the group's appearance in 2001. "We found the fest to be an uplifting event for ourselves in its many-faceted celebration of all that is good from the island of Ireland and all things to do with Irishness," he affirmed. Reynolds was appreciative to find an audience "willing to listen and enthusiastically enjoy" the young singers' performance. He took his comments even beyond the strictures of the festival in talking about a joint appearance of his group and the Irish Fest Youth Choir. "I know that lifelong friendships have been made during our stay in Milwaukee, to the enrichment of understanding and recognition of the differences that make us all part of the human race," he philosophized.

Contacts made during the festival have proven valuable on many fronts. Milwaukee musician and fest volunteer Kristina Paris organized several benefit concerts of Irish music for peace action causes, combining her love of Irish music together with her passion for a more peaceful world. "I can truly say I feel very welcomed as a person who has not descended from Irish ancestry. I think there must be some hidden part in there somewhere because it is such a huge part of my life," said Paris, who is of German heritage.

"Since the first time we played the festival, we've become friends with a lot of the volunteers and the organizers. They've had us over at their houses for Super Bowls, taken us out to lunch and put us in contact with other venues in the area for gigs. The people at the Irish Fest Center have been great to us," asserted vocalist Patrick Murphy of Gaelic Storm.

The festival has affected others in many special ways. "Impact" comes in many packages. Milwaukee Archbishop Timothy Dolan can still remember the awe and emotion of walking into the Marcus Amphitheater for the 2002 Mass, with its standing-room-only crowd of more than 14,000 of the faithful. He had been appointed archbishop in June of that year and not yet installed. Dolan had wrestled over whether it would be appropriate to say the Mass before officially sitting in the archbishop's chair. "But then I thought, no, I made the commitment, I'm looking forward to it, I don't want to let those people down. I need to go. Am I ever glad I did!" he recalled. The tumultuous welcome, the beautifully enthusiastic liturgy, the participation of the people, the songs, the responses at Mass and chance to be able to speak about the importance of faith in Irish heritage remain uppermost in Dolan's mind. "I still say that was a providential moment and part of one of the greatest weeks of my life. I've been archbishop of Milwaukee for two and a half years and I still meet people who say, 'We were there at Irish Fest that first year.' I'll never forget that and I just remember speaking from the heart and being so overwhelmed at the warmth and the welcome and the interest of the people there."

The Fans Can't Stop Talking

Dedicated festgoers are not noted for holding back on suggestions or complaints. Comments usually focus on which bands played, should have played, should not have played or hopefully would be playing. Other letter writers -- while they may complain of the lack of Guinness or Jameson's on the grounds, crowded restrooms, full parking lots or kids blocking their views of the stages -- usually begin their notes by saying how much they enjoyed everything.

"I drove from Kansas City, Missouri, and attended every day and night you were open. Having traveled to various Irish festivals throughout the United States, I thought I'd seen it all. I have never been so impressed with a line-up such as the one you had this year. In fact, I am planning my vacation around Irish Festival (sic) 2000 and am bringing as many friends as I can."

Brian Price, Missouri

"I appreciated the opportunity to experience the world's largest and grandest Irish festival. The authentic food and music provided an ideal environment for festive recreation and celebration. I would like to commend you on an extremely well-planned celebration of Irish heritage."

John F. Weishan, Jr., Milwaukee County Supervisor

"Thanks for the opportunity to experience Irish culture and to see the many fine groups on the music scene...Irish Fest gets better every year! What a grand job you do!"

Chicago fan

"Just a note to say what a wonderful weekend the 1985 Irish Fest gave us...The standard for the music is high, please keep it so...Next year, we'll build a family vacation around Irish Fest."
Pat Kovalcheck, Vanderbilt University, Nashville, Tennessee

"Twelve of us made the annual pilgrimage to Milwaukee and we just wanted to say thank you for the most wonderful festival we've ever experienced...Milwaukee and Wisconsin should feel justifiably proud of Irish Fest. It is truly an unrivaled celebration of culture that epitomizes the best of our ancient traditions."

Eamonn O'Loghlin, manager of field and retail communications, Hallmark Cards, Toronto, Canada

Green Tie committee members Kathie Daily & Kay Noel

Paddy visits the Milwaukee County Courthouse

The archbishop even passed on a good word about Irish Fest to the pope, the late John Paul II, mentioning the event in an *ad limina* report, a required rendering to the Holy Father of an account of the state of his archdiocese. "I spoke about the vitality of the Catholic faith and the deep appreciation for ethnic heritage and roots (in Milwaukee)," Dolan said.

Through all the growth, the festival has stayed on course and continues to be run in a businesslike manner, even if by means of mostly volunteer help. It has achieved a comfortable balance -- with an occasional hiccup -- between the need to be profitable and the need to share its success in a way that benefits the community-at-large.

Irish Fest has long reached out to that community, whether by working with Mothers Against Drunk Driving to encourage responsible fun or by donating tickets to dozens of social services and charities such as Transitional Living Services, Ranch Community Services, Veterans Administration Center, St. Ann's Home for the Elderly, the Salvation Army, National Multiple Sclerosis Society, Children's Outing Association, the Guest House of Milwaukee, Wisconsin Association of the Deaf and the St. Francis Children's Center. Such largess is appreciated. A thank-you letter from the Jewish Vocational Service of Milwaukee (now the Milwaukee Center for Independence) in 1989 overflowed with wobbly, but enthusiastic, handwritten thank-yous from its mentally and physically challenged clients. The Milwaukee County Sesquicentennial received a gift of $3,000 from the festival in 1985 and other civic activities have also received funding gifts.

Yet, establishment of the Irish Fest Foundation demonstrates most vividly what the event is doing to ensure an enduring legacy. The idea of a grant-awarding body had been around for a while but became front and center as the festival became more successful and profitable. Festival directors were always concerned about how to respond to the question of "Where does the money go?"

For many years, funds were deposited into a reserve to protect the festival against bad weather. When the festival board decided to go ahead with establishing a foundation, it received the volunteer help of Attorneys Tim Riordan and Larry Burnett from the Milwaukee firm of Reinhart-Boerner-Van Deuren.

When the Irish Fest Foundation was launched in 1994, it initially had a board of six, which has since grown to nine. Members meet quarterly to consider grant applications, with decisions made by all board members present. Approval is based on the project's merit and how it relates to the Foundation's mission to promote Irish culture and Irish education and support community and civic activities. Governmental rules prohibit grants to individuals, thus the Foundation can only give grants to eligible not-for-profit organizations.

Most years, it is the goal to expend relatively equal amounts for each of the three major missions. The amount given is measured by the earnings on the conservative investments made the previous year so the Foundation committee typically knows the approximate amount available for distribution.

Since it does not draw upon the principal, the future of the Foundation is secure. Irish Festivals Inc. has given a portion of its proceeds each year to the entity so it can grow. One proviso -- since part of the mission is to support the interests of Irish Fest -- if the festival were ever in peril, it would be able to draw upon the resources of the Foundation as needed. As the festival gets larger and more costly, it will be an ongoing challenge to keep revenues ahead of expenses, the Foundation directors realize.

Irish Fest is committed to ensure the continuance of the Summer School, the Foundation, the School of Music and the John J. Ward, Jr., Irish Music Archives. These operations will continue to pursue the original goals of Milwaukee Irish Fest: that of preserving and promoting Irish culture.

The Foundation has never gone out to actively raise funds, although it has accepted a few donations. It has granted awards each year since its inception. Amounts distributed in 1994 were $2,750; 1994-1995, $9,632; 1995-1996, $10,300; 1996-1997, $11,750; 1997-1998, $12,717; 1998-1999, $11,284; 1999-2000, $17,330; 2000-2001, $18,300; 2001-2002, $25,250; 2002-2003, $19,400; 2003-2004, $29,800. The festival often reaches far beyond the Irish scene with its largesse. As an example, it provided a special donation of $10,000 for 9/11 charities. In 2005, it granted $30,000, including a $5,000 gift to the Catholic Relief Services to aid tsunami victims in Southeast Asia and $5,000 to assist those affected by Hurricane Katrina. During President McAleese's visit, the Foundation established the Mary McAleese Annual Grant, which pledges $5,000 a year for five years to causes of peace and social justice which are consistent with her goals as Irish head of state.

Among local recipients have been *Conradh na Gaeilge*, Milwaukee Irish Arts, Shamrock Club, UWM-Foundation, Irish Cultural and Heritage Center, Alverno Presents, Pier Wisconsin and local dance schools and *feisiana*. The Foundation's generosity extends internationally, as well. Receiving funding have been the Willy Clancy Summer School, the Francis McPeake School of Music, Omagh Youth Choir, Paddy Clancy Memorial Scholarship Fund, the Tommy Makem International Song Fest

Irish Fest Foundation presentation to Muiris O Rochain and Harry Hughes, founders of the Willie Clancy Summer School in Miltown Malbay, Co. Clare

The Impact

131

More Fanfare!

"Is the festival coming to Baltimore?"
Maryland patron

"My daughters and I had a terrific time on the grounds -- especially when we tried some of the dances (Boy, were we ever lousy but it was fun!)."
Patti Gorsky, executive director,
Make -A-Wish Foundation of WI

"What a great Fest! God blessed us with great weather so we could enjoy the beautiful music, dancing, fellowship and displays. Each year is a better year and I cannot wait again until next year!"
Sister Ann Catherine Veierstahler, SCSJA

"As I shook hands with the crowd, I was impressed by the number of people that had traveled from out-of-state to be present, which speaks very well of you in planning Irish Fest. I thought the entertainment was very good. The green derby I got at the Fest is sitting proudly on display on a shelf in my chambers."
Justice Roland B. Day, Wisconsin Supreme Court,
Madison, Wisconsin

"You can be proud of the world-class music and attractions that Irish Fest offers. Congratulations on a job well done."
John O. Norquist, Milwaukee mayor (1988-2004)

"I have been in this country for many years and live in a community that does not have a substantial Irish community, so I had never been to anything quite like the Irish Festival. My husband and children really enjoyed the music and entertainment, and looking through the shops that were set up, and I just loved it."
Nancy Kukia, Columbus, Ohio

"We were part of the Celtic Canine display and we had a blast. Both my dog and I are exhausted after two fun-filled days but the memories of the event make the exhaustion worthwhile."
Lisa Schaitberge and Beacon, her Irish water spaniel,
New Munster, Wisconsin

and the Arts Council of Northern Ireland. It is always a thrill for Foundation officials to see the ongoing success of various programs they supported, like the Ulster Project of Greater Milwaukee.

To be able to donate to projects and causes in the name of Irish Fest volunteers is a real privilege, agreed Colleen Kennedy, Foundation president since 2000. "We can invest in furthering Irish culture and knowledge and in improving our community by supporting non-profit entities," she explained. What makes it extra special is that the Foundation does this in honor of Irish Fest volunteers, who have helped to generate the largess.

With such enthusiasm, it is certain that the legacy of Milwaukee Irish Fest is secure and that its impact on preserving Irish culture will continue to grow.

The contributions of talented Irish Fest workers and dedicated festival fans have expanded widely beyond the event itself and its year-round calendar of activities. Creative individuals have gone on to provide the grunt work in founding and nurturing an ever-growing number of new Irish organizations catering to women, musicians, genealogists, theater fans, athletes and dancers. The city can also boast of its own on-line news publication, the international *The Irish American Post*, founded as a newspaper in 1991.

The broader Milwaukee community thus continues to routinely support parades, recitals, concerts and lectures at area theaters, libraries, universities and related outlets far beyond the realities of Irish Fest. This marvelous mix of activities contributes to a very deep and broad Irish renaissance in the city, the seeds of which were planted by a group of far-sighted friends meeting in a bar back in 1980.

Irish Fest Foundation President Colleen Kennedy presents the seed money to Mary Clancy for the Paddy Clancy Scholarship Fund

Then-County Executive William F. O'Donnell, former County Executive John Doyle and former Milwaukee Alderman Bob Dwyer, 1982

During the opening *hooley* night ceremonies in 2005, deadly storms swirled around Southeastern Wisconsin but Milwaukee was spared the turbulent weather. As the evening's program on the Aer Lingus stage wound down on that Thursday, a marvelous light show appeared over Lake Michigan. It was as if a "cue the rainbow" order was part of the script. The scenario, played out against the backdrop of challenging skies, was symbolic of the festival's 25 years, a timeline replete with highs and lows and a lot in-between.

But mostly the rainbow was a promise that, yes, indeed, there will long be a pot o' Irish Fest entertainment gold secreted in Milwaukee.

The Impact

133

IRISH FEST PRESIDENTS

Ed Ward	1981-1984
John Maher	1985-1987
Jane Anderson	1988-1991
Jerry McCloskey	1991-1992
Ann Comer	1993
Colleen Kennedy	1994-1998
Jane Walrath	1999-2001
Barb Tyler	2002-2004
Ed Ward	2004-

FESTIVAL DIRECTORS

Ed Ward	1980-1991
Jane Anderson	1991-Present

BOARD OF DIRECTORS

Mary Cannon	1980-1984	Barb Tyler	1988-Present
Joe Dowling	1980-1981	Colleen Kennedy	1990-1998
Mark Goff	1980-1981	Coleen Kennedy	2000-Present
Bill Hanrahan, Treasurer	1980-1981	John Gleeson	1990-1993
Bernie McCartan	1980-1984	Julie Smith	1991-2003
Bernie McCartan	2004-Present	Mike Brady	1993-1996
Lorraine Murphy, Vice Pres	1980-1981	Maureen Modlinski	1993-2002
Danny O'Connell	1980-1981	Mary June Hanrahan	1992-1998
Mary Ellen Simet	1980-1984	Dan DeWeerdt	1994-1997
Ed Ward	1980-Present	Julie Bolthuis	1996-2002
Chet Radtke	1981-1984	Bob Harrold	1996-1999
Tim Casey	1981-1984	Joanne Woodford	1996-2004
Mary Otto	1981-1986	Maureen Tyler	1996-2000
Mary Otto	1992-1998	Mike Boyle	1997-2000
Derry Hegarty	1981-1981	Mike Dahm	1997-Present
Jerry McCloskey	1981-1992	Tom Rave	1998-2001
Mike Brady	1981-1986	Kathy Wood	1998-5/2001
Jane Anderson	1981-1991	Jeanne Cissne	1999-2002
John Maher	1981-1987	Katie Ward	1999-2002
Jackie Kane	1984-1988	John Moriarty	2000-2002
Cecelia Grinwald	1984-1990	Tom Tiernan	2001-Present
Sarah Dann	1984-1988	Tom O'Connell	2001-Present
Tom Barrett	1984-1999	Joe King	2002-Present
Pat Brennan	1985-1992	Gail Fitzpatrick	2002-Present
Tom Kennedy	1986-2002	Kathy Rave	2002-Present
Jack Early	1987-1994	Lori Dahm	2002-Present
Jane Walrath	1987-2004	Tadhg McInerney	2002-Present
Kathy Mallon	1987-1990	Maricolette Walsh	2003-Present
Pat Russell	1984-1997	Kevin Kendellen	2004-Present
Pat Russell	2000-Present	Donna Brady	2004-Present
Ann Kerns Comer	1987-1993	John Killoren	2003-Present
Chuck Ward	1988-2003		

In the Beginning...

Paula and Bob Harrold get religion

McFest Time

Dance!

139

Erin Go Bragh

CULTURE • MUSIC • HERITAGE

irish fest foundation
SUPPORTING THE GOALS OF MILWAUKEE IRISH FEST

Soft Days

On the
March!

144

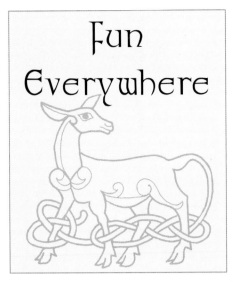

Fun Everywhere

Druids visit the Gaelic Gathering

Breakfast with Nick McFest

St. Patrick's Day Miller Free Ride promotion

Frank DeGuire and Sue Riordan at a Green Tie Event

Irish Fest Bocci Ball team at Festa Italiana

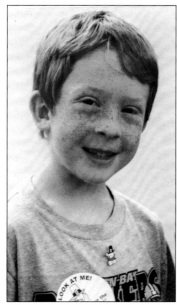

Kid Time!

Irish

Rovers

Back row: Bill Margeson, Brian Doherty, Liam Clancy, Eugene Byrne, Maura Byrne, Mick Moloney, Aine Ó Cuív, front row: Kim Clancy, Dianne Coish, President McAleese, Martin McAleese, Joannie Madden, Tommy Makem & Minister Éamon Ó Cuív

Finbar McCarthy

Brigid's Cross

Bill Crowley directs Summer School class

Tom Sweeney leads Summer School song session

Musical Madness

Irish folk song legend Frank Harte

Tommy Makem, Ed Ward and Liam Clancy

Milwaukee Mayor Tom Barrett and Tommy Makem

Tommy Sands

Marianne Mikush Fisher

Jerry (Andy) Anderson

Steve Wehmeyer of Gaelic Storm and
Tom Tiernan

Bridget Jaskulski and son Nathan

Chuck Ward

Ward Family: (l-r) Chuck, Caitlin, Jack, Cathy, Ed, Jane (Cagney), and Colleen

Ed Ward welcomes President Mary McAleese and her husband Martin

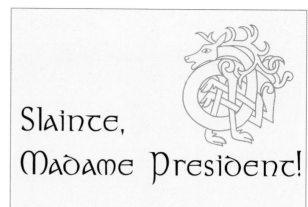

Slainte,
Madame President!

Ulster Project host family kids meet President McAleese

The Spirit of Galway contingent with the President

154

Commemorative quilt by Bonnie Hardt presented to President McAleese

President McAleese aboard the *Denis Sullivan*

Mary Alice Tierney & Colleen Kennedy on the alert

Rip O'Dwanny and Fr. John O'Brien

Fred Curtis, Waterford Crystal cutter, presents chandelier gift to Jane Anderson

Bill Heenan, Steel Recycling Institute

1981
Karen Lehre

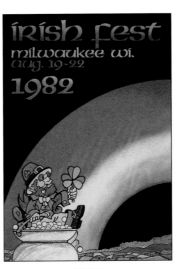

1982
Wayne Peterson

1983
Mel Teiss

1984 -1986 Suite of three years by McDill Studios

1987
Ron Ceszynski, Designer
John Neinhuis, Photography

1988
G. Coffey

1989
Ron Ceszynski

1990
Steve Slaske, Artist
Tommy Makem, poetry

1991
Bette Leyre

1992
Jennifer Knaack

1993
Aaron Boyd

1994 Poster Winner

Mary June Hanrahan, Ken McCance, and Veronica Ceszynski

1994
Ken McCance

1995
Paul Fleming

1996
Scott Taylor

1997
Julie Hartman

1998
Raymond Strange

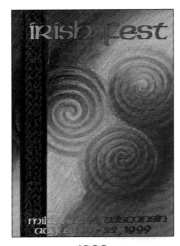

1999
Paul Ward

2000
Bill Korinek

2005 Poster Winner

2001
Melissa Arnold

Michael Versatig with Carrie and Pat Benway

2002
Nick Sanders

2003
Tina Eveland

2004
Andy Sharlein

2005
Michael Versatig

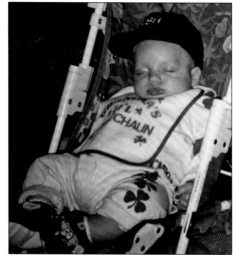

Until Next Year...

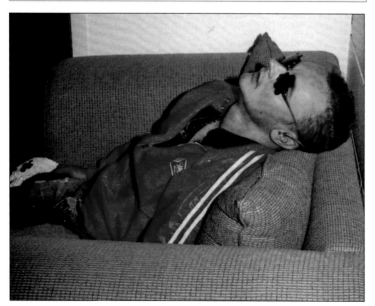